MW01255216

How to Teach Mental Skills to Athletes

Confident, Calm, and Clutch Coaching Companion: The Ultimate Guide to Coaching Mental Toughness
Foreword By Jack Smithlin

Valerie R. Alston MA CMPC

Alchemy Publishing Group

First edition 2023

CONTENTS

FOREWORD BY JACK SMITHLIN

The Mind Game. What an important part of athletics, and life for that matter.

So many coaches, and parents, are now beginning to understand the value and importance of the mind game, better known as Sports Psychology.

While listening to elite athletes after an important win or an outstanding performance, win or lose, you'll often hear them mention how unbelievably important it was to have a positive mindset. It's not just being physically prepared, but mentally as well. Sometimes they'll even speak about being in the "zone."

I have been coaching almost 50 years, and I've witnessed the results of athletes and teams having a positive, powerful mindset. Now, you may ask how that is possible. Watch an athlete that has absolutely no control over their emotions, then an athlete that does. The difference is obvious.

See, the difference between the great athletes and the not so great athletes is not in their ability to play the game, it's their understanding that the brain is a powerful tool and that it can be utilized to help their skill levels skyrocket.

I've been studying the mental side of athletics for many years. I have witnessed athletes who can't control their emotions and those who carried their past poor performances forward into their next games. Sometimes, after having failed, they're not even able to compete in their next events.

I recently discovered a book that teaches young athletes about the skills and practices of the mental game, Val's first book, "Confident, Calm and Clutch."

In all my years of reading sports books, attending conferences, clinics and seminars on the topic of Sports Psychology, I never found a book written specifically to instruct coaches and parents how to present this topic to their athletes and children. And then, Val wrote her second book, addressing exactly that topic.

After reading "Confident, Calm and Clutch," I responded to Val's request to give her my opinion of the book and to tell her about my background and coaching experience. Val and I connected by phone and text, and even discussed possible workshops and exercises for my college team. Then Val asked me to read and comment on her newest book, "**How to Teach Mental Skills: Confident, Calm, and Clutch Coaching Companion - The Ultimate Guide to Coaching Mental Toughness**" I had almost nothing to offer. Like her first book, this one is a masterpiece. Just brilliant. I have never come across a book written like this. If I were to use a cliché here, I would have to say that "The Coaching Companion" is the Goose that Laid the Golden Egg.

Why? Because it provides insight that is crucial to learning and understanding everything there is to know about mentoring and teaching your athletes. It provides explanations, exercises and worksheets. There is also an extremely valuable chapter titled, "The Book Club." When you talk about tools for teaching, this book is it. It has it all.

"The Coaching Companion" is a must read. You will be doing your athletes, and yourself, a great injustice if you do not incorporate the information and teaching techniques into your coaching repertoire. Add this book to your library and tell everyone about it.

I always research the authors when I read a new book about the Mental Game. So who is Valerie Alston? If possible, she is probably overqualified to have written this book. Val possesses a BS in Kinesiology and a Masters in Mental Health with a specialty in Sports Psychology, and is a Certified Mental Performance Consultant (CPMC). But here's the icing on the cake... Val was an exceptional Division One softball athlete, living and learning through her academic and athletic experience - what I call life's best teacher. So when reading "The Coach's Companion," understand that it was written by an expert on the topic. Someone who learned it, experienced it and now teaches it. Can't get better than that!

In conclusion, I would have to say that it is an honor having been asked to write the foreword to "The Coaching Companion," a book on a topic of which I am so passionate.

"How to Teach Mental Skills: Confident, Calm, and Clutch Coaching Companion - The Ultimate Guide to Coaching Mental Toughness" is so educational and fun to read. A TRUE MASTERPIECE!

Jack Smithlin

New Jersey City University Assistant Softball Coach/Hitting Instructor

Fair Lawn High School Athletic Hall of Fame Coach (Soccer, Softball, Wrestling)

44+ years of coaching experience

Host of a Sports Talk radio show on Long Island, WGBB 1240, and frequent guest on the Legendary Rick Wolff's Sports Edge Show on WFAN

Get a free gift with purchase!

Get access to 3 video tutorials for using the lessons in this book. These tutorials expand on the instructions in this guide.

https://www.valstoncoaching.com/coach ingcompanion_freegift

Scan the QR code to receive an exclusive surprise.

https://www.valstoncoaching.com/coachingcompanion_freegift

View From the Coach's Box by Greg L. Alston

What is The Purpose of Coaching Young Athletes?

Many parents become youth sports coaches because others can't or won't commit the time and energy to manage a team of young athletes. We take on this task whether we have any idea how to be an excellent coach. After all, it is just a bunch of kids playing a game. How hard can it be?

I started out coaching my son's little league team and made every single mistake a new coach could make. I barked at kids when they messed up. I rolled my eyes when they made an error. I pushed them to get better. I worked them hard in practice. My focus on the outcome removed the joy from the game. It is no wonder that my son quit playing and hates baseball to this day.

But God has a sense of humor and she gave me a second chance when my daughter began playing fast-pitch softball. I quickly learned that my coaching had to improve dramatically if I was going to build a highly competitive team. I learned that if a young girl doesn't think you like her, she won't play well. Each team member needs a defined role and opportunities to excel. I learned that the players you pick for your team must buy into your style of play and fit within your system. I learned to stop over-coaching and let them play the game their way. And I learned that my actions, attitude, character and behavior had a tremendous impact on our team's success.

Each player has physical talent and mental/emotional talent. When a player is confident that you believe in him/her, their physical talent can perform at its best. Physical talent won't succeed if the player lacks confidence, can't handle pressure, or fears failure.

As a new coach, I'd react negatively when a player made a mistake. Although I didn't speak, the player could sense my dissatisfaction. When the game got close, I would get nervous and upset, and my team could sense it. I would get angry over terrible calls and my players could feel my frustration. I could tell that my behavior was not helpful, so I changed. My attempt at being fun and unbothered was unsuccessful. It felt like I didn't care about the outcome at all and we lost our competitive drive.

The light bulb went on for me when I decided that coaching was a means of teaching my players the life skills they needed to thrive. The game served as a crucible for us to learn important skills like hard work, passion, excellence, teamwork, and trust.

I developed a set of core values to serve as the unifying force for my travel teams. I committed to helping each player become the best they could be. I ensured everyone knew their team role and played with enthusiasm. We played with great defense, solid pitching and timely hitting. I spent enough time with each player, so they knew I believed in their ability.

Helping young athletes excel was my focus as a coach, not being a spectacular coach. My teams never had the best talent in our age bracket, but we competed hard and routinely beat higher ranked teams. I would observe other coaches tightening up in the late innings of close games. That's when I knew we'd win. On my teams, we loved close games. I'd repeat that this is our kind of game in the dugout. We love to play tight games. We love to break their hearts. Our motto was Play Hard, Have Fun, No Mercy. And my teams won consistently for eight years in a row with one national championship with 6 other top ten finishes and one 11th place finish. We were successful because we adopted mental toughness and resilience as our team ethos long before most teams ever knew what it meant.

Your role as the coach of a team is essential to the team's enjoyment of the sport and your ability to win games. I got to spend over ten years on the ball field with my daughter and some amazing young ladies. They taught me more than I taught them. Here are some coaching tips for your journey to becoming a brilliant coach.

1. It is not about you. It is about them. No coach has ever won a game, although many have cost their team a win.

2. Concentrate on the process, not the results. Teams often lose games before they begin because of inadequate mental and physical preparation.

3. Don't coach physical technique during games, it causes brain freeze and prevents performance. Coach mental and physical skills in practice to improve technique and approach. Let them relax and play during games. Assess what to focus on after games.

4. Use your powers of observation and knowledge of each athlete to keep their mental game focused during games. A word of encouragement can turn a game around.

5. Take command only when you need to. Over managing stifles team growth.

6. All eyes are on you. Show the enthusiasm, positivity, and energy you need to keep your team focused when it matters most.

7. Avoid holding team meetings after a loss, except to thank them and set a future meeting.

8. Practice is not a game. Some people are practice superstars but less effective in games. Other's performance in games is better than their practice performance. Let your players play their way in and out of a starting role.

9. Both stars and role players are necessary for team success. One player does not deserve all the glory nor all the blame.

10. Do not allow your team's parents to undermine your athlete's success. You should never tolerate parents demeaning or talking bad about someone else's child. We should always resolve any disagreements in private between the adults without the child present.

Special Topic #1

It is important that you be 100% objective when your child is on your team. Don't give them advantages they don't deserve. But don't hold them to higher expectations than anyone else either. My daughter, Valerie, was never the best athlete on my travel teams. She was a skilful player, but lacked the foot speed to be a superstar. I began the recruiting season by targeting players of her caliber or better. I figured that if she was the worst player on my team, we would have a great team. The competition for play time was fair and wide open. She had to earn her way onto the field. By the end of the season, she was always a starter and key to our success. Because she knew I did not guarantee her anything; she developed amazing work habits and maximized her skills as a player. She played a variety of positions in order to gain play time. Her hard work paid off in college, where she played second base for 3 years after starting as a catcher.

Special Topic #2

There are two basic styles of coaching competitive youth sports teams. Some coaches seek to improve their teams by finding better players and recruiting them away from other teams. Their strategy is to poach the best players they can find so they can win as many games as possible. The coaches are doing little to improve their players. They choose kids who are already at the peak of their performance. Loyalty isn't their strong suit. The team will play with a group all season but add pick up players for big tournaments.

The second style of coaching is to select athletes with the potential to be excellent players and then coach them up to become competitive. This coach looks for talent, attitude, drive and work ethic. The coach helps players exceed their expectations. This is a more fun and fulfilling way to coach young athletes. Only one team wins the national title at the year end. The absence of a title is a failure if you judge yourself by titles. When you measure your success as a coach by the growth of your players, then every team can achieve their goals.

Molding a group of kids into a winning team, especially those rejected by other coaches, is a special joy. Two of my teams earned a 1st and 4th in National Championships, however, my favorite team of all time was the group that finished 5th. No-one expected us to win. And winning got harder when our top pitcher got injured in the first inning of our first game. With only two losses by one run to the second-place team, the kids finished 5th. I've never been prouder of a group of athletes.

But sports is the test ground, life is reality. As a dean and professor at two graduate programs, I met many young students training to be pharmacists. In my research with over 5000 students, 70% were high school or college athletes.

Contrary to popular belief, athletes are superior students. They perform better in school and work, have superior social skills, and are more confident adults. In almost every aspect of life, athletes perform better than average students. Coaches can improve players' lives by teaching them important skills.

Valerie's books and training develop mental skills for success in sports and life. You don't have to be an expert on Sports Psychology. Just follow the outlines she gives you to help your team perform better and learn to love the challenge of competing.

God bless you for devoting your time and effort to the young people in your charge. They won't realize how important it was until much later in life. Their parents may not thank you. But you are doing the right thing. Part of your mental skills development as a coach is to realize that you can only control what you can control. Use your energy, enthusiasm and passion to teach them how to overcome adversity, block out distractions and compete. Contrary to the prevailing mindset in society, competition is an essential part of life. If your athletes don't learn to deal with failure and overcome obstacles, they will never achieve their full potential.

Greg Alston

Father, Educator and Head Coach Orange County Batbusters 10U, 12U, 16U, 18U

INTRODUCTION BY VALERIE R. ALSTON

This book is the Coach's Companion for my best-selling book "Confident, Calm, and Clutch". Thank you for helping make that book such a rousing success.

If you remember what a textbook is, this is its teacher's edition. This book will give you the strategies and tactics to implement the mental toughness skills and drills outlined in the original book. If you don't have a copy of that book, you should probably order one today so you can see the student's and coach's edition.

Many of you have reached out to me to get more information about how coaches can integrate mental toughness training into their practice plans. That is exactly what this book does.

Several of you inquired about obtaining copies of the book for your team. The process is simple. Contact me and I will show you how to order multiple copies at a 33% discount shipped directly to your home. Both the original book and players' journal are available for order. Go to the Resources page at the end of this book to find the order link.

This companion aims to give coaches the tools to help teenagers develop the mental toughness skills they need to thrive in life, not just in their sport. There is a mental health crisis in youngsters in our country today. While we can debate the root causes, far too many teenagers have depression, anxiety and other mental health issues. Modern life has exposed them to several layers of social pressure from friends, school, media and their social media accounts. I can't change any of that. You can help them build the skills they need to thrive in spite of these factors by developing their discipline and mental strength in their sport.

Youth sports have changed over the past few decades. The professionalization of many youth sports has occurred. Getting on the right team and being noticed by college coaches has turned the game into a job. It is no longer enough to make the "All-Star" team from your league. Being on a championship tournament team is now required. Many of these teams draw players from long distances, so they are no longer a group of local kids playing together.

Many coaches spend more time recruiting top players than developing players to reach their potential. And because of the driving distance and constant pressure to play games, many teams don't practice skills as often as they should. The ability to learn from mistakes and improve skills at practice is missing. Athletes in these environments often think they have to be perfect. And because of this pressure, they become the opposite of confident, calm or clutch. And that's causing some problems for teens.

My mission is to help teens develop a different perspective. If they learn to focus on the process of competing, rather than the outcome of winning, something magical will occur. If they focus on becoming the best they can be, rather than worry about getting recruited. They will build strong friendships, strengthen their character, and develop the work ethic that will catapult them to success in life.

I want young athletes to pursue their goals in a healthy way, building mental toughness and resilience. That's why I wrote my book, Confident, Calm & Clutch and why I have also created this companion. In a perfect world, I could coach each of your athletes individually. My years of training and experience would help them all. Time limitation prevents me from doing that.

So my challenge is to help you serve as the Mental Toughness Coach for your team. I am confident we can do this together. If you have any issues, I'm here to help you.

Mental Toughness can help your athletes join an elite travel team, play in college, or earn more playing time and maybe even go pro in their sport.

If you want to:

1. See your athletes walking tall with confidence and self assurance.

2. To be awed by how they handle pressure.

3. Be inspired by how well they perform under pressure

4. Prevent them from feeling overwhelmed and overworked.

5. Assist them in shedding the societal pressure to be perfect.

6. To inspire them to keep striving for excellence and enjoying the process.

7. See your athletes get back to playing loose, having fun, and performing well.

And allow them to grow and thrive in all aspects of their lives. This book will be helpful to you. I want to help your athletes get the tools they need to become mentally tough. With your help, they will learn to handle the stress of playing sport at an elite level.

Sport is a metaphor for life. Life doesn't always go well. Sometimes it goes amazing. Sometimes life throws you a curveball. There's a lot going on. And if we can teach kids how to handle those moments in sport more effectively, they can handle them in life as they move through it.

I want to introduce you to the fundamental process that I consider, to be the essential elements of building mental toughness. Teaching your athletes these three things can help them be mentally tough and successful.

It's a very simple process. Technically speaking, it's three steps. But, the nuance of doing each one of those steps isn't always easy.

The Three Important Steps

Discover

The initial step is to **DISCOVER** the barrier. Help your athletes look below the surface and ask themselves what's going on. What is working? What is not working? They have to discover and learn about themselves to build self awareness.

Build

After becoming self-aware, they can learn specific skills and tools from Confident, Calm & Clutch to **BUILD** their mental toolkit. What tools and skills do they need to overcome their challenge? How do they tweak their behavior so that they build a pattern of success rather than a pattern of failure?

Apply

And then once they've built that tool, they need to **APPLY** that tool in a productive and meaningful way to affect their performance.

It's a simple process: **discover, build, apply.** Achieving that is harder in the real world. The goal of this Coach Companion is to give you concrete tools and ideas to help your athletes **discover, build, and apply.**

The goal is to help you stop walking on eggshells around your athletes. You don't have to feel a sense of hopelessness and helplessness as you see your athletes struggle with their confidence and sense of self worth plummet. It's awful to feel that as an adult. Feeling emotionally drained and saying the wrong things that affect athletes' confidence and self-worth is not enjoyable for coaches.

This book can help you reduce anxiety about your athletes' future by teaching you how to help them build mental skills for confidence.

Coaching is challenging when your team is struggling, and you're unsure how to assist. It doesn't have to be like that.

The aim of this book is to equip you with one or two additional techniques to facilitate this process.

In this book, you will get:

Expert Advice

I provide several specific ways to use the Confident, Calm & Clutch book with your team. Read and discuss one chapter per week like a homework assignment. Use my tips to lead conversations about the mental side of sport. It doesn't require a master's or PhD. By asking the right questions with my help, coaches can improve their athletes' mental toughness.

Easy to Use Drills

Don't just read about mental toughness, implement it into your coaching. Add "Confident, Calm & Clutch" drills to your practice or game strategy. These easy-to-use drills work for coaches at any level.

Special Note to Coaches

THANK YOU for doing what you do. Many coaches don't get the appreciation they deserve. Many of you are volunteering or receiving little compensation. Your time, effort, and energy are invaluable to the young athletes you influence daily.

There are aspects of coaching that you love, otherwise you wouldn't do it, but I know it can be a thankless job. Many parents and kids don't always appreciate the sacrifice it takes away from your own family, job, vacations, etc.

I want to start this section by saying that I appreciate you and what you do. Coaches from my past, like you, helped me develop into who I am today. You're human, like anyone else. You make mistakes and have bad days. But your willingness to keep showing up to help your athletes makes you outstanding in my book!

Thank you for dedicating your time to coaching young athletes. If no one else has said it to you yet, I APPRECIATE YOU!

I'm very excited by your purchase of this coaching companion for one important reason. It tells me you care about trying to be the best coach you can be. It tells me you want to help your kids as best you can. The best thing you can offer your athletes is being honest with yourself as a coach and knowing your strengths and weaknesses.

I'm excited you read "Confident, Calm & Clutch" and want to help build mental toughness in those you coach and that you wanted a few more ideas on how to do that. This coaching companion offers you specific coaching strategies. You don't need to be an expert to develop mental toughness and resilience in players. This book offers guidance on incorporating mental toughness and resilience into your athletes' training.

If you want to develop confidence, calmness, and clutch ability in your athletes, model these traits as a coach. It is vital that you practice what you preach to the best of your ability. Perfection is not required. You are human too. But if you can apply the principles from Confident, Calm, & Clutch then you can lead others through applying them to.

Below are some tips that I recommend you do as a coach to best model and live the principles of Confident, Calm and Clutch. Do your best with what you have. Recognize it takes work. Use the tools and skills in your own life to better serve your athletes.

Coaching Tip Number One

If young athletes want to play their sport at an elite level, they need good coaching and to learn the sport's fundamentals. Don't focus on playtime, focus on coaching and skill development. If they receive good coaching, they will get better. Assure your athletes that they will get to play when they work hard to refine their skills. Clearly communicate about how athletes can earn play time and assist in skill development.

Coaching Tip Number Two

If you become a coach for your child's team, it is essential that you award playtime based on performance and not on nepotism.

Your child should understand they need to earn their playtime. If they don't, they will be missing an important life lesson and their progress will stall. In adulthood, you will rarely get anything for free. You must earn jobs, pay raises, and opportunities. The goal is to teach children the value of hard work through earning their playtime, which will benefit them in their adult life.

Coaching Tip Number Three

The process of success is more important than outcomes. Outcomes matter. But focusing only on outcomes can make athletes feel pressured and break the rule of controlling what they can.

There is a correct way to approach and execute any athletic skill. Doing the skill right will lead to more success. Reward the correct approach and process and your athletes will improve. Focus only on the outcome and your players may get discouraged and fail. Long-term benefits come from applying the right effort, strategies, and skill execution. If they prepare well and use the right processes, they will set conditions for excellence.

Actual outcomes (wins, losses, batting average, runs scored) are often outside of their control. The right processes will help an athlete improve faster. Your goal needs to be understanding their process and helping them do it correctly. Coaches should reward athletes who have the right preparation, effort, skills, and strategy. Over emphasizing outcomes can discourage preparation. Coaches who don't support young athletes when they fail can prevent mental toughness growth. Let your athletes know that your support is not based on their performance.

Coach Tip Number Four

Resist comparing your individual athletes to other kids on the team. Each child has his/her own strengths and deficiencies.

Discuss your athlete's strengths and weaknesses and identify needed improvements. Help them with the drills. Teach your athletes to work hard and control what they can control. Encourage them to practice the right mechanics of movement, and they will get better. Help them see the joy in getting better and improving their craft.

Coach Tip Number Five

Read this entire book. If you still need help after you've finished the book, contact me. No two teams have the same issues. I provide personalized coaching and tailored programs to help you, help your young athletes achieve their full potential. Teams might need an unbiased third-party to help them build better communication and teamwork. I will help you if you need it. *(See the resource page for more details)*

Coach Tip Number Six

Don't always tell your young athlete what to do regarding their sport. Ask them questions to uncover what they think. Some sample questions are:

"What do you want to achieve?"

"Do you want to learn how to be calm in clutch moments?"

"Would you like to reduce stress during the game?"

"What are your goals for this season?" Then listen to the answers.

Confident, Calm, & Clutch explained the knowledge and drills your athletes need to become mentally tough. Help your athlete explore the options by reading the book together and discussing each chapter. Be a coach, not just a teller. Serving in the assistant role can also be valuable at times. We assume we know what is happening with them when we tell.

Coaches are not always aware of their athlete's internal state. Technique and behaviors are visible, but intent is not always apparent. It's a better practice to start by asking, than assuming. As it relates to mental toughness skills, this guide will give you tips on how to have these conversations.

Coach Tip Number Seven

You are a performer, too! Make decisions and communicate with your team effectively by using mental skills the way athletes do.

Make sure you are also practicing the mental tools discussed in Confident, Calm, & Clutch. Be transparent with your athletes that you are also working on mental toughness. Model the vulnerability that you also make mistakes and are learning and growing as a coach. I realize this can be scary. Many coaches think this will cause their athletes not to trust them. Vulnerability quickly earns athletes' trust, according to research. They see you being willing to admit mistakes and it helps them see that they too can admit mistakes. It helps create the psychological safety to learn and develop. (more on this later)

Not every mistake or doubt needs to be shared as a coach. Some of those are better suited for your adult peers and fellow coaches. Acknowledging observable mistakes in front of your athletes can show mental toughness and build a strong team culture.

Coach Tip Number Eight

You have your own mental and emotional "baggage" that you bring to the field. Your thoughts and feelings on the game and what it means to be a good teammate are part of your baggage. You have your own emotional experience after big wins and tough losses. There are behaviors that your athletes engage in that annoy you and drive you nuts. Managing parents, kids, umpires all while trying to be calm and coach your athletes is tough.

Being an effective coach requires you to be aware of that "baggage" and how it affects your decisions and behaviors. It's not good or bad, right or wrong, but it is your reality. Knowing yourself well makes coaching and developing athletes easier. This means that you too should apply and practicing the skills discussed in Confident, Calm & Clutch.

Coach Tip Number Nine

Coaching is hard work. It can feel overwhelming and draining. Don't overlook the importance of having fun. Figure out ways to have fun with your athletes. Incorporate silly shenanigans in practice occasionally. Take part in the drill your athletes are doing and take an at bat off your pitchers. Have music at practice. Let your athletes teach you a silly TikTok dance. Create fun bets with your team (if they go undefeated at a tournament, you'll wear a dress for the whole next practice or shave your head or sing an embarrassing song.)

Remember to have fun with coaching too! Don't take yourself or the sport too seriously. It's important to focus during "work" but also important to have fun. Find something about coaching and the sport that brings you joy, then do it!

Coach Tip Number 10

Coaching is a skill, a science and an art. Coaches can always enhance their skills. To become a better coach, devote time to increasing your knowledge and skill level based on your coaching level (rec, travel, high school, etc). Take advantage of opportunities to learn from experienced coaches at clinics or conferences. If you don't have spare time & money, read! I provide recommended resources for being a great coach at the end of this book.

You can use my Discover, Build, and Apply method to improve your coaching skills, even if you can't buy new books or go to clinics. To become a better coach, create a reflective practice by taking notes and journaling. Ask yourself what's working and what's not.

Willingness to learn and grow is key to improving coaching skills. It will also help you recognize and develop your own personal philosophy towards coaching. Find your own way. You can maintain your authenticity and still be an amazing coach. That is the art part of coaching.

If you would like some help to improve your own coaching skill and abilities, you can reach out to me or join the Coach's Corner Community. I'd be happy to help you in the Discover, Build, Apply process as it relates to your own coaching development. Head to the resource section for options.

CHAPTER 1: DISCOVER

Coaches can assist athletes in understanding what affects their performance and personal life, as well as coping with stress.

Self-awareness is one of the biggest gifts you can give people. Helping athletes build the capacity to reflect and understand themselves is vital to success. According to successful individuals, being self-aware and adaptable is crucial to becoming great.

"I think self awareness is probably the most important thing towards being a champion." - Billie Jean King

"Self-awareness gives you the capacity to learn from your mistakes, as well as your successes, and enables you to keep growing." – Lawrence Bossidy (former CEO of General Electric)

It is the tool, the mechanism for everything else. Other tools or tips become useless if athletes lack self-awareness. They don't understand how to use it, because they don't know themselves. One of the biggest gifts you can give people as a coach is teaching your athlete how to be more self aware.

Learn From the Past Don't Judge It

Teach them to treat everything as a learning opportunity. To learn from the past and not judge it. Reflecting on the past is valuable in any context, like school or sports.

The important step in the reflection process is to reflect without adding judgments. Abandon the concept of right and wrong. Instead, focus on what happened, what worked, and what needs adapting, tweaking, or change in your approach.

Here are some ways to increase effectiveness. First, acknowledge you are a human being. You've got your own emotions, beliefs, and values interpreting the thing your athlete just did or is dealing with. To the best of your ability, you want to set those emotions, beliefs, etc. aside and try to be a neutral and partial sounding board for your players. They need a safe place to reflect. If they know you will jump down their throat for admitting they weren't paying attention during the game, they are less likely to share that and get help for it.

Ask Reflective Questions

The most important thing you can do to help facilitate the **Discover** process is to ask effective questions. This serves three vital functions for your athletes down the road.

First, encouraging reflection improves skill retention and transfer for athletes. Teaching a mental skill that helps calm nerves during a big at-bat can also help a student relax before a big exam in school.

Mental Skills are Life Skills!

Second, by asking reflective questions, you are promoting independent learning. Giving a man a fish feeds him for a day, as the saying goes. If you teach a man to fish, you feed him for a lifetime. By asking good questions, you are teaching your athletes to engage in the learning process for themselves. You are teaching them **how** to discover, not just doing it for them.

Third, by asking questions, you are helping build rapport and a relationship with your athletes. You are getting to know them, how they think, how they respond, how their brain and body works. You are showing them you care about their experience and them. Athletes won't care what you know until they know that you care about them. By involving them in a reflective discovery practice and showing that their input matters, you are saying loud and clear, "I care about you!"

When asking questions, be patient and wait for the answer. Don't fill the quiet space with your own thoughts. Don't answer before they have finished what they wanted to say. If you don't listen to their answers, asking questions is a waste of time.

Basic Principles of Effective Questions:

- **Open-ended questions** - a response should require more than yes/no. It should invite exploration and reflection.

- **The question should have a purpose** – What's the purpose of the question? What topic do you want to discuss? Knowing your athlete, what's the best way to approach this topic? Prepare for the conversation or reflection. Then craft your question to guide the conversation in that direction.

- **Seek descriptive information not just evaluative information** - evaluative information is often outcome based (did you get a hit, did you catch the ball, did you hit your spot), whereas descriptive information is more about the experience of performing the task. Things like: How did that feel? Walk me through your process.

- **Make your questions future focused** - asking things like "what can you do differently next time?" Your questions should stimulate reflection, curiosity, creativity, and new possibilities. By focusing on the future, you also help the athlete move away from judgment (good, bad, right, wrong) thinking and more towards solution focused thinking.

- **Watch out for assumptions** - be careful and watch out for assumptions. For instance, after a game asking, "what did we do wrong today?" that's assuming something went wrong. "What did we do right today?" Again, that's assuming something went right. Being general avoids biasing the conversation or their reflection.

The most important thing is to ask yourself: "How do I get them to reflect on their process, thoughts, emotions, and feelings?"

Questions like:

- How did it go today?

- How do you feel out there today?

- Can you share your reflections on the event?

- What did you learn?

These types of questions invite conversation and exploration. That's the coach's most useful tool. One, you're removing your own assumptions of what their experience was. You weren't in their body or head. You observed outward behavior, but you don't necessarily know what the root cause of that behavior was.

You might have interpreted an event as a lack of hustle. Perhaps they were unsure of what to do. And so they just froze. If the player was overwhelmed and confused, coaching them like they were not hustling won't help.

Questions help you ensure that you're coaching and mentoring in the right direction. You are also learning from them. The aim is to guide their discussion towards things they can control.

Redirect Focus to the Controllable

They can own the process and grow by focusing on controllable factors. Ignoring uncontrollable factors like teammates, umpires, field conditions, and weather. Yes, there's stuff to learn from these moments, when uncontrollable factors influence outcomes. But it's out of your control. For instance, if it was raining, and that affects play. You can't change the rain. Making sure you practice in the rain a bunch will not be the best use of the limited time you have with your team. Focusing on things they can control boosts optimism and confidence in their ability to improve their performance. It's not all up to chance.

Alright, let's look through a couple of scenarios.

Scenario 1: Your athlete has made an error that allowed the other team to score. And the other team won the game. And now it's after the game. You want this kid to learn and don't want them to feel judged. We all make mistakes. Start the conversation without being judgmental. Use questions like: "When that error happened, what was going on for you?" or "Walk me through that play." You are encouraging them to reflect on the situation by removing any form of judgmental tone from voice. The player knows he/she screwed up. You don't have to point that out. Let them know you want them to learn from their mistake, not beat them up about it.

Remember that a game, especially a youth game, doesn't matter in the overall scheme of things. I know that's hard to hear. But it doesn't. It has no bearing on real life. Yes, games matter at some point. If you are getting paid to coach and your livelihood depends on wins, winning becomes important. But youth sports should be about growth and development. As they become adults, it doesn't matter whether they won a game when they were 14.

As adults, our stakes may differ from the athlete's. In these cases, it is essential that we not be judgemental. We don't want to add more pressure to the athletes. Removing judgments can help build confidence and competence in this athlete.

Every athlete will be slightly different. Some need a pat on the back, some need a kick in the butt, and some need a hug. It is your job to adjust your style to match what the player needs to absorb the message. And the guts of the message is, we have agreed on a process. How is that process working? What can we do to get better? How can I help you excel?

The reflection questions become a very important coaching tool. In the situation above, let's suppose your athlete responds with "The ball took a bad hop and ricocheted off my shoulder. That's why I made the error. It's the stupid field's fault".

Now this informs your next coaching questions. You could ask, "Is there anything that you could have done differently, so the field didn't become a factor in the play? How can you incorporate that next time?" Hopefully, the athlete responds with something like, "I could have charged the ball." By simply inviting exploration, you are allowing the athlete to refocus on what they have control over. You help them figure out how to be better next time.

If your coaching observation was that the athlete was indecisive about charging the ball, causing them to get stuck on the in-between hop. Now you can offer feedback to help them correct that mistake.

If you corrected the athlete without asking the reflective question, imagine the outcome. You might provide correction / coaching for the wrong thing. Now your athlete tunes you out because they know your feedback was incorrect. Asking first helps you focus on the right thing.

And the truth is sometimes athletes mess up. The best players in the world make bad plays. Sometimes the reason something happens is that it did. And no correction is necessary. Don't project unreasonable expectations onto your players.

Scenario 2: An athlete is agitated after the game because they didn't perform as well as they thought they "should". When you check in with them, they say, "I'm bummed because I only went 1-3 at the plate. I didn't catch that ball in the outfield in the 3rd inning and I should have caught it".

I say "should" because sometimes athlete's expectations don't match with reality. As a coach, it's acceptable and expected to hold people to standards, that's fine. Athletes, especially younger ones or perfectionists, often set strict and unrealistic standards for themselves.

If their "should" means that they want to go 3-3 every game or catch every fly ball in their direction. Well, you might have to give them a reality check like, "Even the pros getting paid millions and millions of dollars can't do that. If they can't even do that, why should you?" The first thing you can do in these situations is make sure their "should" is reasonable.

Even if they didn't play as well as they thought they "should," you want to invite reflection like: "Why do you think it didn't go the way you wanted it today?" Again, they're going to give you some answers, and you can offer advice and suggest corrections. You could ask, "what did you think should have happened today? And what impeded your ability to do that?"

The aim is to help them gain control over their future performances through reflection. And if you can help them develop this reflection ability, they will change the future.

Special Note: Until your team is comfortable with this reflective process after games, it is probably best not to start this dialogue after a defeat. Emotions may run high and anyone who messed up will be reluctant to engage. This could cause more harm than good. Be observant and assess your team's willingness to listen. It may be best to have this conversation at your next practice when the emotions have evened out.

And once again, get to know your players and understand how to approach each player in a way they will accept.

Chapter 2: Build

After the Discover process, now you have to help your athletes **BUILD** their mental tool kit. Use Confident, Calm and Clutch tools to help them out. I'll share specific ways to incorporate the drills into practice later in the companion.

Most coaches and players spend 90% percent of their time in their sport focusing on the physical and technical elements of their sport. The mental aspect is as important as the physical, but they focus less on it.

As a coach, if you're not practicing or developing the mental side with deliberate tools and skills, then you're leaving it up to chance. You can train your athlete's minds the same way you would train their bodies. All it takes is deliberate practice.

All practice is not equal. Deliberate practice is purposeful and systematic. While regular practice might include mindless repetition, deliberate practice requires focused attention and is conducted with a specific goal in mind. Mindless repetition is the enemy of growth.

Growth Mindset and deliberate practice yield higher improvement rates. We don't all have equal potential. Genes and talent play a role too. The goal is to help everyone improve, no matter their predisposition.

What makes practice deliberate? Two things, focused attention and feedback. Focused attention refers to having a purpose or goal for the repetitions that you put in. Feedback provides information for athletes to make corrections and adjustments.

Special Note: Practice sessions are the time to critique and challenge your athletes, not games. Drill and automate your athletes' technique during practice. During games keep their mind clear so it can react at game speed. With mental toughness, you must be careful not to allow negative self talk, fixed mindset excuses, or poor reset processes to go unchallenged. Redirect poor thoughts just as you would correct a physical skill.

Deliberate practice requires a simple process.

You must understand the overall outcome that you are trying to achieve. Then you need to break that outcome down into its component parts. Once you understand the component parts, you can then design your practices and drills to develop those techniques and skills. Start with foundational movements in isolation, then gradually move to integrating that technique or skill into a more game-like scenario. In the Army, they call this the Crawl, Walk, Run approach. The neat thing is that this approach works for both mental and physical skills.

When developing your practice plan consider:

- What are your overall goals? What are some specific performance goals you are working on? - Overall goal: Finishing 1st in the league. Performance goal: All batters swing at good pitches and make solid contact in 80% of at bats.

- Which performance components require improvement? - Hitting with 2 strikes, hitting off-speed pitches

- What drill or exercise can improve that component? - 2 strike drills, pitch tracking drills, balance drills, work with batting coach to work on off-speed every lesson.

- Do you have a customized development plan for each of your athletes? Not everyone needs to work on the same thing.

Train your mental game with the same intention as your physical, technical, and tactical training.

Even if you're not an expert on mental skills, you can ask questions that guide your players to cross-talk and share tools they are already using. Asking about what worked, how to repeat it, and how to adjust if it didn't build their skills. You can help build mental tools by guiding the conversation towards self-discovery, even if you don't have expertise in mental skills. As a person with more life experience than your athletes, you can offer suggestions. I will discuss this process thoroughly in a later chapter.

In my experience, these two mental tools are the most effective for athletes. The first mental tool / skill that every young athlete needs is a **Growth Mindset.**

Those with a growth mindset believe they can learn and develop skills and abilities. The growth mindset leads to behaviors that improve athletes' skills and abilities.

Athletes with growth mindset:

- Are open to facing challenges.

- They're able to handle setbacks and failure because they

acknowledge that it's a learning opportunity

- They receive feedback and coaching better because they don't feel threatened by it

- They react better to their teammates who are doing better than them currently because they're not threatened by the success of others. Instead, they're inspired by the success of others.

- They give more effort because they recognize that effort is the key to mastery

As a coach, if you can help foster this simple mindset, it will change many outcomes for your athletes who aren't already in the Growth Mindset.

How do you foster the Growth Mindset as a coach?

It's important to emphasize progress, not perfection. Ask them before every practice what success looks like for you today? How do you / can you grow today?

Every player on your team is in a unique position or at a different developmental stage. Players don't all have to be good at the same things. That's why you have a team. Encourage athletes to define success based on personal growth, not comparisons with others.

Help them define what a successful practice or a successful game will be for them today. What are the indicators of success? Help them define it in aspects of the game or performance that they can control, so we can measure their effort and strategy against observable data. Initial stages of the process require more time and effort because of a lack of expertise. Many people define success based solely on outcomes, not their process. If it is unrealistic to have every player share with you, ask each person to write in a journal, notebook, index card.

Coaches can use this for post-practice or post-game reflection with their team. At the end of a game or practice, you can ask everyone "based on your individual definition of success, how did today go?"

This process creates the expectation that we will face challenges. Practice helps us improve by identifying mistakes and weaknesses, so we can fix them for better future performance. Growth-focused athletes maintain the right mindset and improve continuously.

Another tool you can use to foster a Growth Mindset is to give quality feedback. There are many research-backed benefits to providing quality feedback (praise and criticism). Effective feedback not only helps you build the Growth Mindset in your athletes, but it has three distinct benefits.

1. **It enhances performance.** Praising success helps to repeat it, correcting failure helps to improve performance.

2. **It is essential to the learning process**. Without feedback, learning is less efficient in gaining skills. Which is why it is an essential ingredient of deliberate practice.

3. **It enhances motivation.** Athletes who know how to replicate success or learn from failure increase their level of competence. Competence is the belief that they are capable of completing the assigned task or skill. This matters in motivation. In fact, it's one of the three basic psychological needs that we have as humans (more about these later). When an athlete feels competent to execute a skill, they are more motivated to try it in games, practices, etc.

So what can you do to ensure the feedback you give builds a Growth Mindset and develops physical and technical skills?

Follow these principles for Effective Feedback:

- Be **specific.** Provide detailed information about what behavior, process, or strategy worked and what didn't.

- Make it **timely.** Give feedback soon enough for easy recollection. Be mindful not to give feedback too soon, either. When athletes are still experiencing negative emotions, they tend not to receive feedback well. Do your best to find the sweet spot.

- Be **goal-oriented.** Your feedback should clearly help your athlete grow, develop, or repeat a successful action.

- **Provide purpose.** Provide your reason and intent for giving said feedback. For example, "I'm trying to help you get better at hitting with two strikes."

- Make your feedback **collaborative.** Involve them in the conversation! Use the principles of effective questions from the Discovery process even as you give 1:1 feedback.

For Example:

Jimmy had a successful at-bat against a tough pitcher, fighting off many tough pitches, taking the count deep, and making solid contact with the ball. You might provide feedback between innings that sounds like:

"Hey Jimmy, great job staying focused on that at bat. I love the way you battled. I saw you fighting off those tough pitches until you got a good one to hit. That was a great at bat. Using that same approach at the plate makes you a tough opponent. What boosted your focus before this at-bat?"

Example 2: After watching your pitcher walk 3 batters in a row.

"Hey Susie, what's going on? (After getting her input) It looks to me like you're trying to aim the ball instead of just sticking to your mechanics and throwing it. What would help you right now stop aiming the ball and just play catch with your catcher? (get a bit of dialogue) Okay, that sounds like a good idea. Pick a particular spot on the catcher's glove to throw to. Try throwing to the pocket's cross stitch and see if it works. Take a deep breath. Let's get after this next hitter."

Adjust your collaborative feedback based on the player's emotions or actions. If she responds differently, you would hopefully coach differently.

Super Powerful TIP for Coaches:

The opposite of a *Growth Mindset* (skills, talent and abilities can be grown with time, effort and practice) is the *Fixed Mindset* (skills, talent and abilities are fixed at a certain level and won't get any better). The most important word you need to learn to teach Growth Mindset is the word "YET". When an athlete says, "I can't hit the curveball", or any other Fixed Mindset lie, you simply get their attention and say, "You mean you haven't learned how to do it, **yet** right?" The word yet means, I can't right now, but I will. Any athlete comment that begins with **I can't**, or **I will never**, requires your immediate attention. You should respond with **YET**.

It is ESSENTIAL to ensure that athletes understand that greatness takes time to build. Just because you can't do something "right now" doesn't mean that you won't be able to do it in the future. It is vital to understand this concept. I hate to break it to you but you don't know what your athletes are capable of. Their true athletic potential is often many years down the road once their bodies have fully matured and grown. As a coach, we **never** want to put limiting beliefs on athletes. You can of course give them realistic assessments of their **current** skill level. That is your job as a coach. But please refrain from making judgments about their future ability. You don't have an all seeing eye, you don't know what their future potential holds, so please don't act like you do. Encourage the right mindset, provide quality feedback and let their work and effort dictate their future.

Self-Awareness and Voicing Needs

The second key skill that you should help your athlete **BUILD** is the ability to understand and voice their own needs. Asking your athletes "how can I support you today? What support do you need for me today?" lets them drive the learning process and give you a clearer picture of their personal goals or needs that day.

They may request help with a struggle or express a desire to work on something. You can suggest or create a drill for them to practice the ability.

Sometimes your athlete might say, "it's been a rough day/week. I just need a hug". Often, your role as coach is just to support them as a human. When softball/baseball practice isn't their top priority, a hug can be the best remedy. Let them know you care, send them out to the cage/field and let them be.

Sometimes we forget young people don't need constant coaching. Occasionally, they might just need some space to breathe. Be with friends doing something they enjoy. Or not "striving" for anything.

To better understand your athletes' mental and emotional state, it is important to train them to communicate their needs. You should always uphold standards and team rules/norms. However, sometimes you might need to throw out your practice plan because your team is too overwhelmed, tired, or beat down to take any more "correction". Sometimes they just need to have a bit of fun or experience short-term wins to build back their confidence.

The other reason building athletes' ability to understand and voice their needs is that it facilitates their own discoveries. It helps them develop the ability to solve problems on their own. Obviously, you're there to support them and give them help as needed.

It's a crucial skill for everyone, not just athletes. Teach them to identify what they need to improve and they will find their own solutions. This helps them understand there's no one right way to learn, develop and grow.

Helping athletes with a Growth Mindset and communication skills sets them up for success. Give them effective feedback that emphasizes progress over perfection, remind them that growth takes time. It won't happen overnight. Encourage them to ask for what they actually need.

CHAPTER 3: APPLY

The last piece of the Discover, Build, Apply process is to help your athletes **APPLY** their performance plan. Whatever you have helped them discover and build as it relates to being confident, calm or clutch, they should apply it regularly in practices and games. The drills section has specific ways to apply skills, but guiding athletes to use them is key for success.

Consider this tale of two athletes.

Athlete A consistently "just wings it". It's clear that their actions lack intent. They just fly by the seat of their pants in games and practice.

Athlete B who shows up and says, "coach here's what I'm working on" and they do it very deliberate during their pregame or practice. They have a game plan for their at bats.

In your experience, which athlete outperforms the other?

The athlete who prepares deliberately usually outperforms the one who doesn't. When you help athletes with their intentionality and purposeful use of skills (physical, mental or emotional), they are APPLYING. They'll develop effective habits and processes, increasing their success rate.

Helping your athletes understand the value of preparation and its impact on success is essential. You have probably heard the famous John Wooden quote, "failing to prepare is preparing to fail." As a coach, think about what your team actually needs physically, mentally and emotionally to be at their best before, during and after performance. Then plan your strategies around that and you will help your team be more successful. But more importantly, they will learn the how to become Confident, Calm and Clutch.

Think about one of the common problems athletes have: transitioning into practice or game mode. Athletes might be unfocused or chaotic if they come straight from school without shifting into practice mode.

I'm sure you have experienced this too as an adult. One moment you're shifting tasks, the next it's time to leave. You hurry home to change and collect your gear for the field. Maybe you quickly inhale a protein bar or something as you drive. Then you attempt to get mentally present to lead a productive practice. The same transitions you deal with, your athletes have to manage as well.

For yourself, one of the most helpful things you can do is have your own pre-practice or pre-game routine that gets you mentally and emotionally ready to coach. Helping your athletes/ team make the shift into the right mindset will ensure they can be confident, calm and clutch. You can assist them to ensure they focus and prepare themselves for work or competition.

One of the best things that you can do is help your team or your athletes develop a pre-performance routine. It can be brief. They should intentionally switch their focus and energy to the right mode depending on the type of performance, whether it's practice or game.

Think deliberately about how you prepare your team in the pregame warmups. Think about what you currently do. Does it allow time for personalization for athletes to do their individual stuff to get ready for games?

Do you have any type of practice routine that transitions your athletes from school, home, long drives, etc. into practice mode? Consider using the "conversations to build mental toughness" chapter as a mechanism for transition.

Special Note for Coaches

Be transparent with your team. Here are the processes I am working on. Here are my goals for developing my coaching skills. In order to help our team thrive, what do you guys think I need to do better? I see that our pregame routine needs to be better. How can we improve? If you engage your team in the process of success, that process includes you as well. When they know you appreciate feedback, even when it is critical, they will see you modeling the behavior you want from them. Let them see you trying to grow and they will be more likely to buy in to your plan.

Game Plan

Besides mental and physical skills, the other thing you should help your athletes APPLY is a game plan. While this may seem obvious to you, young athletes often overlook the importance of mental preparation and planning for their opponent. That based on who you are getting ready to play and what you know about them, they can strategize how to maximize their success.

Teach your athletes how to meet the challenges they will face, whatever their skill level. This helps them focus on what they can control and to put their energy and efforts in the right places.

I worked with a cross-country runner who had difficulty reaching competitive times. She had the ability and had previously run those times, but was struggling with her confidence after a poor performance. I asked her, "what is your race plan? How do you get ready to run?" And she looked at me like I was crazy. I asked a few more questions like; do you have a pace you are trying to run at? Do you run the first mile that same as the 3rd, etc? She responded with, "I never really thought about it. I just warm up and go run".

Well, you can probably guess why she was struggling. She had absolutely no plan for how to run the race she wanted. Just getting her to think through that and create a plan helped her immensely. She habitually started too fast and had no energy at the end. I helped her develop a simple race plan and a better pre-race routine and she starting doing much better, running at her normal race times.

In baseball and softball, having a game plan for your at bats or pitching is crucial.

Athletes need to have intention or a plan for achieving the outcomes they want. Success doesn't just happen by chance. This is why successful pro athletes or teams study game footage. They are trying to learn as much as they can about their opponent so they can build a game plan to set them up for success.

Even if you don't have access to game footage. Develop effective game strategies by analyzing opponent's playing style. Obviously, any game plan might need to shift as real world competing conditions change. But having a starting point about how you are going to attack this race, hit against this pitcher, attack this team's hitters, etc. makes it easier to succeed.

I would recommend that the game plan should not just be technical and tactical. It should include all elements of the sport but also help them be prepared for distractions and common problems that are likely to occur.

How will they deal with a bad call, poor weather, a mistake or error, etc?

Helping an athlete build a plan for these types of moments allows them to have more confidence because they feel prepared. When they feel prepared to use specific strategies to overcome these things, it allows them to manage their nerves because they know what to do.

These are the simple things that you can do to help them **APPLY** skills they've learned from the discovery and build process. Whatever they've come up with, hold them accountable to actually doing that thing. You will help them play well and have confidence, calm and ability to be clutch while they do it.

You do not have to be mental skills or sport psychology expert to lead your athletes in the Discover, Build, Apply Method. Athletes learning what works for them is valuable. It's best for athletes to write their discoveries to remember them later. (see the journaling section for more tips)

The next few sections will give you specific ways to implement the process into your practices and games.

Chapter 4: How to Use Conversation to Build Mental Toughness

You don't need to be a sport or performance psychology expert to talk about mental and emotional aspects of performance. You don't need to have all the answers. Your players can learn from each other. A good coach provides the platform for discussing the mental and emotional aspects of sport both in practice and games.

The process can be simple for non-experts.

1. Ask your athletes to focus on a topic during training. Share your reasoning for your choice so they can understand and improve their own solo training.

2. After the training/practice discuss the relevant topic you chose. Encourage athletes to keep what worked, share ideas, and make adjustments for things that didn't work.

3. If they are doing more than one iteration of a task/drill/workout, follow the same sequence for each iteration so they can hopefully see progress.

There are a few keys to success that will help you use this process.

- **Keep it simple** - focus on one topic at a time.

- **Foster curiosity and generate conversation** - the goal is to get athletes cross talking and discussing how these topics play out for them. One of the greatest advantages of generating discussion like this is to help players realize they are not ALONE. Many of their teammates are having similar struggles and challenges. Young people can find it freeing and affirming.

- **They can learn from each other**, no need to be an expert. Let the athletes share ideas, personal strategies or brainstorm together what they think might work. This helps build their ability to discover, build and apply when they are working out / training alone.

- **Lend Your Experience**-As a coach, you have experience helping other athletes and as an athlete yourself. You have game knowledge and often specific training /education on the topic. When relevant, add your expertise. Contribute to the discussion while focusing on the goal topic and helping athletes Discover, Build and Apply.

The topics can come directly from the Confident, Calm & Clutch chapters or you can use generic topics relevant to high performance. The list below is not exhaustive, but corresponds to essential ingredients of mental toughness and resilience. Use these topics/questions to discuss the mental side of performance after any training or game event.

The list of topics/questions below can help you create an effective discussion among your team about the mental aspects of performance.

Sample topics and corresponding questions:

Thoughts / thinking patterns - What kinds of **thoughts** were you having (get specific) and how did they affect your performance? What would you change for next time? How would you do that?

Emotions / emotional control - What kinds of **emotions** were you having (get specific) and how did they affect your performance? What would you change for next time? How would you do that?

Confidence - What was your level of **confidence** (self and team) before starting? How did you manage doubts/fears etc? What is your level of confidence now? If it changed, what caused it?

Focus- What were times you had trouble **paying attention** to the task at hand? How did you deal with it? (if they were ineffective) What tool or strategy could you have used to refocus or stay focused?

Energy Levels - What was your **energy level** before starting? Was it effective? How could you have increased your effectiveness?

Nerves / Anxiety - How well did you manage your **nerves** during performance (get specific examples)? How could you have been more effective? What strategy could you use to better manipulate your **energy/nerves** to match the demands of the task?

Goal Setting - What was the **goal** of this task/performance? Did you/we meet it? Did you/we stick to the plan?

- How will you adjust your **goal** for the next drill/practice/game? How will you adjust your plan to accomplish that **goal**?

Mental Rehearsal/Visualization - Did you **mentally rehearse** before performing? If yes, how? What did you imagine and was it helpful?

Pre-Game Routine - Did you use a **routine** to prepare? How did it work for you? What would you change? (could also use for pre-at bat or pre-pitch)

Control the Controllables - What was something **outside of your control** that affected your performance? How did you deal with it? What **was in your control** and how did you manage it?

Growth Mindset - Did you maintain a growth mindset (believing you can get better at this skill / drill / task) throughout this session/iteration? If not, how could you prime a **Growth Mindset**?

Motivation - What was your **motivation** level before starting the practice/game? What happened to your motivation during? After? What did you learn about your own motivation and how can you use this in the future?

Examples of what this could look like.

Example 1: let's say that you are preparing your team/players to do a long conditioning workout. Looking at the list of topics, you decide the motivation seems like it would apply to a long conditioning workout. So you decide to prompt your team by saying something like:

"Today is going to be an endurance workout. We need to get your bodies ready to play multiple games in a day. The goal is to keep working without stopping. Our focus of the day is going to be **motivation.** I want you to pay attention to your level of motivation throughout the workout, and we will discuss it when we finish. Pay particular attention to when your motivation changes and what you do to keep going."

After the workout during the cooldown, you ask the motivation questions from the list above

- What was your motivation level before starting the task/training?

- What happened to your motivation during? After?

- What did you learn about your own motivation and how can you use this in the future?

Example 2: You are working on a drill or game scenario you know will be difficult. It's an area of the game your team has been struggling with lately and you know there are likely to be lots of failure moments throughout practice. Looking at the list of topics you think **controlling the controllable** will be relevant for managing the learning process. You could prime your team by saying something like:

"We will work on (insert thing you are struggling with) today and I know we aren't where we want to be **yet**. While we are working on these drills/scenarios, we may struggle a bit. That's ok, that's why we are working on this. I want you all to pay attention and notice where your focus goes during the drill and how that affects your performance."

After you finish the drill/scenarios, you could ask the Control the controllable questions:

- What was something **outside of your control** that affected your performance? How did you deal with it?

- What **was in your control** and how did you manage it?

Leading conversation and drawing attention to mental components of performance is incredibly valuable. But you might find you actually want athletes to learn specific skills, go back to the Confident, Calm and Clutch and pull out the tool that addresses the scenario being discussed. You can also reach out to me to request training in person or via Zoom.

CHAPTER 5: BOOK CLUB

This section provides you with specific discussion questions directed at the main sections of the book. Treat this section like a book club or bible study type conversation. Assign your athletes a certain section of the book to read prior to practice. Then, at practice, you can lead your athletes through a conversation in that section of the book.

As a coach, you can choose which session to cover first. However, I recommend starting at the beginning as each chapter builds on the previous. The book club method is a great way to review Confident, Calm & Clutch during off/pre-season when more time is available. It can also serve as a team building opportunity. Teammates and coaches will learn about each other when discussing book sections.

I planned discussions for 30 minutes, but they may take longer depending on group size and participation. If you have a large team (>10) consider breaking them into smaller groups of 3-5 people. Pose the question that you want them to discuss. Give them 8-10 min as a small group, then have all the groups share a bit of what they talked about. Depending on the size of your coaching staff and parent volunteers, you could have one adult per small group.

This book club style chat lasts 8 weeks if you do one section per week. If you can do 2 sections per week, it will take 4 weeks. Athletes need adequate time to read before discussion. Adjust based on the age/education level of your athletes. Confident, Calm & Clutch is a quick read. If you have a pre-season style boot camp, you could ask your athletes to read the full book and then have one discussion per day of camp. Reach out if you need help implementing this process. (see resources page)

BEFORE STARTING Book Club:

Ensure all athletes have a copy of the book to read at home. (See resources page, access options to the book). Allow athletes to prepare by giving them the questions ahead of time. Athletes can avoid wasting time with the team figuring out their answers and have better conversations. The resource section has worksheets available to send home with your athletes.

Coaches consider it a best practice to inform athletes about the basics and the way to conduct conversations, as well as to share personal intentions for facilitating these conversations. Here are some highly recommended rules/guidelines you should convey before starting.

1. These conversations are designed to help you gain awareness about your own mental toughness challenges related to playing _____ (insert sport). We will talk about these common challenges and how to overcome them using the lessons in the book.

2. It is vital that you read the section before showing up so that you can have a meaningful dialogue with your teammates & coaches.

3. These conversations involve sharing personal stories, worries and seeking our help. It is important that we treat everyone with respect and not judge anyone. What happens in our discussion groups stays in our discussion groups. Do not share or discuss other people's stories outside of this team. (What happens in Vegas, Stays in Vegas)

4. Be willing and ready to talk. To improve at being Confident, Calm, or Clutch, you must discuss and practice it, much like improving hitting or fielding skills.

5. Bring your book with you to these discussions so you can refer to the sections we are discussing.

Add any additional ground rules you think might be helpful for your team/context. For example, what will your rules be (cameras on, etc.) if you need to conduct the sessions over Zoom?

FOR COACHES:

1. Remember, you are facilitating conversation. Get everyone involved and make sure that conversations are staying on track.

2. For any session, incorporate examples from your own team's experience to add value or context to the conversation.

3. To allow for reflection, provide questions in advance to athletes. Not having to come up with answers while with the team saves time and leads to better conversation.

Session 1: Introduction and Mental Toughness Myths

Coach Instructions:

1. Remind your team about the ground rules and expectations since it's your first time leading a conversation.

2. Break the group up into small 3-5 person groups. Ensure they rotate groups each session to work with every team member.

3. Discuss one ASK at a time. Encourage small groups to talk for 8-10 minutes and then spend 5 minutes sharing their ideas with other groups.

4. At the end of each ASK, provide the key summary points and transition to the next ASK.

5. Spend about 15 minutes total per ASK section for this session.

ASK 1: Have you ever had an experience in your sport where your body and mind were so out of whack you couldn't control it and ended up choking? (like Val describes in the introduction to Confident, Calm, and Clutch)

Talk about this moment and its cause to the group.

What did you learn about yourself after you experienced that moment?

Summary 1: Getting nervous, choking, failure moments are normal experiences of playing sports. Understanding past events can enhance future success. The rest of our conversations about this book will highlight strategies you can use to be more successful more often in these moments.

ASK 2: What Mental Toughness Myth do you struggle with the most and why?

Summary 2: Mental Toughness Myths get in our way of building Confidence, Calm and the ability to be Clutch. It's important to know which myths you struggle with or still believe so you can overcome them and set conditions for success.

Session 2: Skill 2 How to Control your emotions

Coach Instructions:

As necessary, remind your team about the ground rules and expectations.

1. Break the group up into small 3-5 person groups. Ensure they rotate groups each session to work with every team member.

2. Discuss one ASK at a time. Encourage small groups to talk for 8-10 minutes and then spend 5 minutes sharing their ideas with other groups.

3. At the end of each ASK, provide the key summary points and transition to the next ASK.

4. Spend about 15 minutes total per ASK section for this session.

ASK 1a: Talk about a time in the past two weeks where your thoughts and emotions hindered your performance? With help from your teammates, practice re-framing the situation (step 5 from reframing drill).

-Each athlete shares an experience, group elects one to work through.

ASK 1b entire group: What did you learn by reflecting on an experience and having your teammates help you think about it differently?

Summary 1: Learning how to think more effectively about the events and situations we experience is a key step in building mental toughness. It's how we build confidence, calm and the ability to be clutch.

ASK 2: Which skill to help you manage your emotions (mindfulness tools, gratitude drill) resonates with you? How do you think you could use it at practice or in games?

Summary 2: Negative emotions are a part of life and the sport experience. The better you get at noticing your emotions by labeling them and using them productively, the easier it will become to manage yourself. Especially when you have failure moments.

Session 3: Skill 3 How to improve consistency and coach ability

Coach Instructions:

As necessary, remind your team about the ground rules and expectations.

1. Break the group up into small 3-5 person groups. Ensure they rotate groups each session to work with every team member.

2. Discuss one ASK at a time. Encourage small groups to talk for 8-10 minutes and then spend 5 minutes sharing their ideas with other groups.

3. At the end of each ASK, provide the key summary points and transition to the next ASK.

4. Spend about 15 minutes total per ASK section for this session.

ASK 1: Taking accountability for your mistakes, decisions, effort, etc. is key to becoming a better athlete. What is one of your personal barriers to taking personal accountability / what excuses to do you make? How has this affected your growth as an athlete?

Summary 1: Taking responsibility for your part in any situation, mistake, etc. can help you take ownership of your learning process. You can't get better if you are unwilling to see what needs improving.

ASK 2: In the next 2 weeks, how / when will use the two drills in this chapter (Get Curious Drill and Consistency Drill) to help you be more coachable or more accountable? Get specific with time, place, context. Brainstorm with your teammates if you need ideas.

Summary 2: The more often you use the Get Curious & Consistency Drills looking back at past events, the easier it will be to use them in real-time. Attempting to be honest with yourself about your strengths and weaknesses will help you grow as an athlete.

Session 4: Skill 4 How to Build Your Champion Support Team

Coach Instructions:

As necessary, remind your team about the ground rules and expectations.

1. Break the group up into small 3-5 person groups. Ensure they rotate groups each session to work with every team member.

2. Discuss one ASK at a time. Encourage small groups to talk for 8-10 minutes and then spend 5 minutes sharing their ideas with other groups.

3. At the end of each ASK, provide the key summary points and transition to the next ASK.

4. Spend about 15 minutes total per ASK section for this session.

ASK 1: Who is currently part of your Champion Support team and how is it working for you? Are there any elements of your support team that are lacking or missing? Brainstorm ideas with your teammates to fulfill those needs.

Summary 1: It is important to feel supported as you pursue sports and life. Make sure you are getting your needs met by friends, family, teachers, coaches, etc. so that you can thrive as an athlete.

ASK 2: What is currently your biggest communication challenge with any member of your Champion Support Team? How can you use the drills in this chapter to help you overcome that challenge? Brainstorm with your teammates.

Summary 2: Improving your communication skills is vital to being a successful athlete and human. Good communication is essential throughout life. Communication is a skill and with practice you can get better at.

Session 5: Skill 5 Building Inner Strength

Coach Instructions:

As necessary, remind your team about the ground rules and expectations.

1. Break the group up into small 3-5 person groups. Ensure they rotate groups each session to work with every team member.

2. Discuss one ASK at a time. Encourage small groups to talk for 8-10 minutes and then spend 5 minutes sharing their ideas with other groups.

3. At the end of each ASK, provide the key summary points and transition to the next ASK.

4. Spend about 15 minutes total per ASK section for this session.

ASK 1: When are the times you struggle most with negative-self talk? What negative self-talk do you engage in? Which of the critical self-talk drills do you find works best for you?

Summary 1: We will all have counterproductive thoughts (doubts, worries, fears, and distractions) from time to time. We are human, that's normal. It's crucial to focus on our strengths, talents, and abilities instead of letting our inner critic bring us down. We become whatever we think we are, so make sure the voice thinks we are capable and worthy.

Ask 2: What helps you the most with having self-compassion? How do you help yourself remember you don't have to be perfect? How do you stop being too hard on yourself?

Summary 2: Being honest with yourself about your faults and mistakes is part of learning and growing. It's how you become a champion. Don't consider yourself a mistake or failure just because of one mistake or failure moment. Reflect on the past but don't judge worth or character on a single event. Learn what you can, then move on.

Session 6: Skill 7 How to Set Goals the Right Way

Coach Instructions:

As necessary, remind your team about the ground rules and expectations.

1. Break the group up into small 3-5 person groups. Ensure they rotate groups each session to work with every team member.

2. Discuss one ASK at a time. Encourage small groups to talk for 8-10 minutes and then spend 5 minutes sharing their ideas with other groups.

3. At the end of each ASK, provide the key summary points and transition to the next ASK.

4. Spend about 15 minutes total per ASK section for this session.

5. **For this session,** consider having the athletes write and turn in their goals to you so that you can review them and use them to guide your coaching choices. This will also give you an avenue for holding your athletes accountable and give you something to check in on throughout the year.

ASK 1: What are some of your personal values that help you thrive in sport? How do they influence you as you try to balance school, sports, and having a social life?

Summary 1: It's important to know what you stand for and how you want to live your life. Do your best to live your values daily, especially as you pursue your goals.

ASK 2: What are some of your big picture goals you have for your sport? What do you want to achieve this year/season?

Summary 2: Having goals and something specific to pursue helps build motivation and discipline throughout the season. Make a copy of your goal and put it somewhere you will see it often.

*If relevant, share how you as a coach will help support these goals and hold them accountable to them. Specify the time and method of your check-in.

Session 7: Quick Fix Tools

Coach Instructions:

As necessary, remind your team about the ground rules and expectations.

1. Break the group up into small 3-5 person groups. Ensure they rotate groups each session to work with every team member.

2. Discuss one ASK at a time. Encourage small groups to talk for 8-10 minutes and then spend 5 minutes sharing their ideas with other groups.

3. At the end of each ASK, provide the key summary points and transition to the next ASK.

4. Spend about 15 minutes total per ASK section for this session.

ASK 1: When will you practice deliberate breathing and how will you use it in games? When will you use the AIR refocus technique?

Summary 1: Breath and refocusing require practice like any other skill. It's extremely difficult to use them in a game under pressure if you haven't practiced and drilled them.

Ask 2: What have you found helps get you the most prepared to play? What do you know doesn't work?

Summary 2: It's important that we all take ownership of the pregame process. You should do things deliberately physically, mentally and emotionally to prepare for games. Our team's warm up is always the same, so add your personal touches. If something we do as a team doesn't work for you, please let the coaches know and we will attempt to make it better.

Session 8: Fixing Common Problems

Coach Instructions:

As necessary, remind your team about the ground rules and expectations.

1. Break the group up into small 3-5 person groups. Ensure they rotate groups each session to work with every team member.

2. Discuss one ASK at a time. Encourage small groups to talk for 8-10 minutes and then spend 5 minutes sharing their ideas with other groups.

3. At the end of each ASK, provide the key summary points and transition to the next ASK.

4. Spend about 15 minutes total per ASK section for this session.

ASK 1: What are you doing to better discover your mental toughness barriers? Do you journal? Why or why not?

Summary 1: Reflecting deliberately can improve sports performance, confidence, calmness, and handling pressure.

ASK 2: What is your biggest lesson learned from our 8 weeks/sessions about building mental toughness? How will you apply this knowledge moving forward?

Summary 2: Mental toughness and the ability to be Confident, Calm & Clutch takes time, energy and effort. It won't come overnight. Small daily steps lead to immense skill growth by season's end. Use the book as much as needed.

*as relevant, discuss how you will implement specific strategies into practice as the coach.

**See suggestions in Drill Section

Allocate 2-3 minutes at the start of practice for each person to write one goal for the day. At the end of practice, take 5 minutes to ask them how it went.

CHAPTER 6: INCORPORATING MENTAL SKILLS DRILLS INTO PRACTICE

Here are some ideas on how to include the Mental Skills Drills from Confident, Calm & Clutch in your practices. Some opportunities arise from mistakes made during practice, while others can be intentionally included in your practice plan. These suggestions give you a starting point as a coach. I encourage you to adapt and expand on the ideas I provide. If you come up with an effective adaptation or new way to apply a drill, please share your idea or successes with the Coach's Corner Community. You can also email me, and I will incorporate it into an updated version of this book.

For the sake of ease and not having to flip between separate books, I have provided the actual drills here for you in this section. Confident, Calm & Clutch has drills not included in the coaching companion. If I excluded a drill, this doesn't mean you can't try to incorporate it. I omitted drills unsuitable for the context or practice. Feel free to incorporate these topics into your coaching conversations. I couldn't envision a way to actually embed it into a softball/baseball drill or activity, but that doesn't mean you won't.

I present the drills in order in which they appear in Confident, Calm and Clutch. Embed them into practice in any order you want. Incorporate certain drills into every practice as part of a routine and others based on need. I will do my best to explain how or why you should incorporate specific drills into your practice plan. If you find you need / want more help, you can reach out to me or join the Coach's Corner discussion group.

My best advice is to add drills based on the needs of your athletes.

What: Reframing Drill

REFRAMING DRILL

Identify a specific event that happened in the past 2 weeks. Select an event from a practice or game where your emotions caused you to act in a way you're not proud of. Then answer the next series of questions about that specific moment.

1. What are the specific thoughts you were having? Write them in your journal. Censor nothing. What actual words, interpretations, thoughts went through your head?
2. How did these thoughts affect you? What emotions did they lead to? Be as descriptive as possible. Try to name the exact intensity of the emotion you were experiencing.
3. What reactions did these emotions cause? Did you throw equipment on the ground or yell at someone? Did it cause a physiological response such as a heart rate spike, tense muscles, eye rolling?
4. Were your emotions and reactions in this situation productive? (helpful) Or counterproductive? (not helpful) Why?
5. If the situation was counterproductive, reconsider the initial event. What really happened? Did you make assumptions that were incorrect? Is there an alternative explanation for what happened? Can you do something different if it happens again? How can you think more effectively next time something like this happens?

This information creates new options for you. Use it to better take control of your mental process and set conditions for success. The more you practice reframing your thoughts, the better able you will be to make adjustments and enhance your performance in real time.

When: The best time to use the reframe drill is when a player reacts unacceptably after making a mistake during a game or practice. This can also be an effective post game conversation for the entire team after a poor game or bad loss. We can use this drill with the Get Curious Drill.

When: Be aware of timing and avoid overwhelming the athlete's system when using this after a mistake. The reframe drill works best in a shortened format as a "coachable moment" for upset individuals. Ask: What's running through your mind right now? Is that working / did it work? How can you refocus your mind and body at this moment?

When emotions are high, you might have to help them reframe the situation, as people can't think productively in this state.

Example:

The batter strikes out looking with runners in scoring position and less than 2 outs. They angrily return to the dugout, slam their helmet and sit on the bench. They ignore teammates trying to support them and refuse to cheer for the teammate at the plate. This player is visibly disappointed. You don't appreciate the way they are acting, but you understand how upset they are. When the inning ends before the team goes back to defense, you pull the player aside. Knowing that you don't want to pile on more "guilt", you remember to meet them with curiosity.

Coach: Jimmy, come here, please. I can see that you are really disappointed / frustrated by your at bat this inning. But it is unacceptable for you to sulk and ignore your teammates who are trying to pick you up the way you just did. Let's figure out what we can do differently next time. During the at-bat, what was going on for you?

Jimmy: Instead of getting the runners in, I fixated on not striking out. I kept saying don't strike out, don't strike out.

Coach: how did that work for you?

Jimmy: obviously not well, I got so in my head I struck out looking.... I'm so embarrassed.

Coach: it's ok to be frustrated. I know you feel embarrassed, but there is no reason to be. We all make mistakes or have bad at bats (reframe) as long as you learn from them, then it's ok. I know it doesn't feel good right now. This feeling will drive you to perform better next time. Clearly thinking about NOT striking out didn't work. What would benefit you the most during your next at-bat with runners in scoring position?

Jimmy: I don't know. Maybe just focus on seeing the ball and taking good swings.

Coach: ok, let's try that next time. Should I remind you about this at your next at bat?

Jimmy: yeah I guess. Please remind me to take good swings at strikes.

Coach: alright I'll do that. Now take a deep breath. Let this one go. Go help your team on defense.

After a game:

Use this to encourage the entire team after a disappointing game and help them see it in a more positive way, especially if they are feeling frustrated. Athletes can turn a loss into a learning experience or use it as motivation to work harder. This might be most important when you have to shake it off and play again fairly quickly.

Example:

After a tough loss with lots of runners left in scoring position or if you were winning most of the game but had a bad last inning and the opponent won.

Coach: Alright, y'all circle up. How are we feeling right now?

Team: Crappy!

Coach: That's fair. I know it doesn't feel good to lose the way we did. And we still need to get ready for our next game. What do you think will happen in the next game if we're still feeling bad about the last one?

Team: It will not go well

Coach: Ok, so what really happened? What got us in trouble?

Team: we let up our intensity and focus in the last inning. We stopped getting ahead of batters, made a few errors and let them score a bunch of runs. That stole all of our confidence and our last at bats. We pressed too much and swung at bad pitches. (There would likely be many answers from many people, but you get the idea.)

Coach: Is there an alternative explanation for what happened? (seek more info if they are leaving out any obvious things that impacted the game) Can we do something different if it happens again? How can we play more effectively next time something like this happens?

Team: We need to maintain focus throughout the entire game. If things go south, we can call a time out. We'll regroup and refocus on the small things we can control.

Coach: Great, I'll help with this. So how do we move forward with the next game? What can we do to shake this off and get ready to kick butt?

Team: HACKY!!!! (Prompt something that you know your team loves to do that will generate positive emotions)

Coach: Alright, take a quick break. Get some food and water. Be back here in 10 minutes for the greatest game of hacky sack ever!!!

What: Mindfulness Drills

MINDFULNESS DRILLS

Practice these mindfulness skills for emotion regulation:

1. Observe your breathing. Set a timer for three minutes and simply notice your breathing. There is no need to be specific. If you can spend time simply noticing your breath, you'll feel calm. When your mind wanders, just go back to noticing your breath.

2. Spend ten minutes coloring. Whether you consider yourself creative, coloring in a coloring book is a great way to focus on one thing instead of getting swallowed up by emotions. Pick something to color that is enjoyable to you. Consider grabbing the kids' menu at the next restaurant you go to remind yourself of a simpler time.

3. Ground yourself. Sometimes our thoughts and emotions get stuck in our head and can't move on. Grounding is a simple technique. Pick three things you can see, hear, and feel. For example, in this specific moment of writing, I can see my computer screen, my keyboard, the bangs in my face as I type. I can hear kids playing basketball next door, the sound of my keyboard, and the music I have playing. I can feel the inside of my fuzzy slippers, my bum on my mesh office chair, and a tight muscle on my back from my workout yesterday. Grounding helps you get out of your head and into the present.

4. Getting outside is a path to mindfulness when you do it with intention. Walk outside with the intention of simply noticing. Observe your surroundings and name the things you see, hear, or smell. You could even consider people watching and trying to imagine their story.

5. If you are feeling powerful emotions, visualize your emotions floating by like clouds in the sky. Close your eyes and imagine a beautiful place that is serene and comforting. Next, imagine that cloud gently passing by. Place one of your troubles on that cloud and watch it peacefully pass onward.

We will focus on Drills 1, 3 & 5.

When: Mindfulness practice is best when used regularly and often. Mindfulness trains the mind to focus on the present moment without judgment. Think of these drills as pushups for our attention. The more pushups you do, the stronger you get. Same goes for focus. The more you practice it (focusing in the present moment without judgment), the better you get at keeping your attention where you want it when it counts.

How:

1. Observe your breathing - this is a great drill to embed into your practice routine. You could add it during warm-up, breaks, and drills transition. Even 2 minutes of intentional breath focus has value. (see simple script in resources) For example, when a team is stretching or warming up, direct their focus to the breath while they

engage in the stretch. Or have them practice a focusing breath before every swing during batting practice.

2. Ground Yourself- This drill is helpful when athletes are stuck in their head or overthinking. Focusing on physical surroundings and sensations brings them back to the present moment. This is useful when you see a pitcher/hitter tensing up or spiraling in a game. You can call a time out and quickly guide them through it (takes 30 seconds). You can also embed this in practice for when players are getting frustrated and stuck.

3. Visualize your emotions - This can also be a great drill to help athletes move on from negative emotions. They can name their negative emotions, visualize putting them on a cloud or leaf, and let them float away.

What: Gratitude Drill

GRATITUDE DRILL

Make a gratitude list or engage in the Three Good Things activity each day. Experience what happens to your attitude. You don't have to conjure grand things to be grateful for. If you like the pen you write with, be grateful for that pen. It could be something you are looking forward to or a nice thing someone did for you. If you're having a bad day and can't think of anything, practice being grateful for the oxygen you breathe, your pet, or your favorite meal. (See resources page for Three Good Things journal options)

Here's how to do it:

1. Reflect on what you are grateful for as you prepare for bed.
2. Write three things that went well today. Draft a reflection using these questions as prompts (pick the ones that apply). Why did this happen? What does this mean to you? How could I get more of this? How did you or someone else contribute to the good thing?
3. Maintain this gratitude journal for at least 1 week. Do your best to not repeat anything you write. Try to find unique things daily.

When: The gratitude drill is a great way to start or end practice. You can use it at the beginning of practice to transition into practice mode. It's a nice way for teammates to connect and build relationships. You get to know your players and it creates positive emotions to help buffer against any negative emotions they may experience from their day.

Make the Three Good Things more specific as a tool after practice. This helps counter the negativity bias and helps your players focus on growth, development, and successes. Again, the goal is to build positive emotion. Each team member can write 3 things in a journal to support their confidence.

How:

Option 1: make it a group conversation. This option is much more free flowing. You can pose the question, "What were some of your good things that happened today and why were they good for you?" Or "what was at least one success, win or moment of growth that you experienced at practice today?

Let athletes take part voluntarily. You are looking for 5 minutes' worth of conversation. Don't hinder celebration and exploration of a good thing when people ask questions after sharing. This multiplies the joy of the individual and allows everyone else to gain more positive emotion. You will need to be mindful of making sure everyone takes part eventually. You shouldn't allow the same 3-5 people to always share.

Option 2: have players write and reflect individually. This option helps players create a list of their accomplishments. Roam around the group so you can ensure everyone is actually writing. I would recommend that you still invite 1-2 people to share after the individual reflection. Pose the same question as option 1.

What: Get Curious Drill

> ### GET CURIOUS DRILL
>
> 1. Think about a recent failure you have experienced. Then use the next few steps to get curious about the situation.
> 2. Slow down: take a moment to tune into your thoughts and assess where you are placing the blame for your current situation. Is it all your fault? Are you blaming everything and everyone else? Are you doing a bit of both?
> 3. Ask critical questions: Regardless of who or what you blamed for a failure moment, make sure you accurately assess what happened. How did you contribute to this situation? How much was someone else responsible? Gaining better accuracy about what is and isn't your fault allows you to move forward with purpose.
> 4. Make a Plan: Develop a plan to improve the factors that you influenced. Then practice accepting the factors that you could not control (weather, field conditions, umpires, refs, other players).
>
> As you practice, the get curious drill for situations that have already happened, an interesting thing will occur. It will be easier for you to use the skill when you experience a failure in real time. In those cases, consider letting, (1) Slow down; (2) Ask critical questions; and (3) Develop a plan; become your process for being coachable in any moment. If you are struggling with the process, involve an objective third party (like a parent or coach) to help you get more accurate or build a plan to improve.

This drill is the Discover, Build, Apply process in mini form. I designed it to run through the process quickly after moments of failure. It is a great reflection process that can enable athletes to be more systematic in their training process.

When: Use as a team or guide an individual through the process after a failure moment. Look for body language showing dwelling on mistakes. I.e. head down, kicking the dirt, quiet and sullen in the dugout, tears, shoulders slumped, no making eye contact, etc.

How: After you witness an individual make a mistake and show any of the signs from above, take a moment to talk with them. Because of limited time in games, you may need to provide more effective thinking to help them get in the right headspace and move on quickly. It could sound something like:

Individual example:

Sarah made an error at 3rd that allowed a run to score. She puts her head down, kicks the ground, and is visibly upset. She has stopped chattering and supporting her pitcher. Call timeout to bring in Sarah for a quick chat, or wait until the inning ends if needed.

Coach: Sarah, I see you are upset about the error. Who are you blaming in your head? What's going on right now?

Sarah: it's all my fault that the run scored. I can't believe I let the ball through my legs. I feel so stupid.

Coach: Everyone makes mistakes. It's okay, the most important thing is to get back in the game and make sure you're helping your team win the next play. If you keep dwelling on this mistake, you'll probably make another one because you're not focused on the game. Play one pitch at a time. No one is perfect. How can you refocus and move on from the mistake?

Sarah: I guess I'll just think about the next play and making sure I charge the ball this time. I know I'll have an at-bat soon. I'll try to make up for it then.

Coach: that sounds like a plan. Keep your head up, just keep playing hard, get your body in front of the ball and your glove down, that's all I can ask of you.

Team example

Coach: All right guys, we let that team back into the game by getting sloppy, not hitting our cutoffs and making bad choices, throwing behind runners. We need to get back in the game mentally. What we should focus on?

Team: Hitting our cutoffs, listening better on where to throw the ball and being ok holding the ball and just getting it back to the circle.

Coach: ok everyone, take a deep breath and let this go. We can't fix the past. Let's clean up our defense. Get some outs and we can get these runs back.

What: Consistency Drill

CONSISTENCY DRILL

1. You can set an alarm on your phone to go off three different times. One in the morning, around lunch and evening.
2. Every time the alarm/reminder goes off, pause and do a short self-reflection. Ask yourself what you are thinking, feeling, and what you notice in your body.
3. Then ask, is this working for me? Are your thoughts, emotions, and feelings helping you to be effective in the moment? Or are they counterproductive and getting in your way?
4. If they are working for you, great, carry on. Keeping doing your thing. If they aren't working, use the drills in the book to change your thinking. You'll be able to build mental toughness if you work at it.

When: This would be a great drill to embed into the natural pauses in practice. For example, anytime you switch drills or transition from offense to defense. For a true mid-performance check, you could yell out "pause" or "freeze" in the middle of a drill and make everyone do a quick reflection. Of course, if you choose to do this, tell them what you are doing so your athletes aren't confused.

How: In this case you are the "alarm". As the coach, you will dictate when your players stop and do the quick reflection. Questions will be the same as before. You might need to remind everyone what to ask. What are my current thoughts, emotions, and bodily sensations? Are they working? Make a rule that players can't step back into the drill until their thoughts, emotions, physiology are in a productive place.

Make it a habit to do this at least once per practice. If you can model the "pause and reflect" model in sport, hopefully your athletes will learn to do it on their own outside of sport. If you are running a long practice 2+ hours, consider pausing the team 2-3 times.

What: Build Your Champion Support Team Drills

BUILD YOUR CHAMPION SUPPORT TEAM

Try these techniques to build your support team:

1. **Analyze your current community.** Look at the people around you and examine your relationships with them. Do you need stronger relationships within your support team? Do you need more people on your team to support you in different ways? Can you communicate effectively with your support team when necessary? Do you need to remove people from your team?

2. **Strengthen connections.** Bonding with friends is important, and you can do so by inviting your friends to take part in activities you're interested in. Doing things you enjoy doing with people you care about strengthens your relationships.

3. **Allow time for conversation.** Actively listen to your friends by responding to what they have to say and staying off your phone. I know this is tough, but it really matters. Through conversation, you will allow your friends to get to know you better.

4. **Join a group.** Groups of people are interested in things you love. You can benefit from a group of people when you engage with them. It is possible to do this online but do some research. Make sure the group works for you.

5. **Be generous to others.** In order to attract quality friends, you need to be worthy of their friendship. Don't be the person who always takes but never gives. One-sided relationships don't last. Be helpful to others and you will discover how quickly you can attract friends.

6. **Show Gratitude.** You can build quality relationships with your team by letting them know how much they mean to you. It's difficult to find good friends, and expressing gratitude is a great way to allow even more friendship. Practice saying "thank you" to people on your Champion Support Team such as parents, coaches, teachers. Remember, they are not your servant they are a willing partner on your team. If a parent rushes home from work and eats dinner in the car in order to take you to practice, offer a Thank You. Most of your coaches are volunteers who give up hours of their lives to make your sport possible. Thank people for their time and effort. It makes your athletic dream possible. If your friend helps you do some of your chores around the house so that you can go hangout, say Thank You. Let people know you appreciate what they do for you. This is an effective way to show appreciation and to build stronger bonds.

7. **Be authentic.** Authenticity breeds inner peace and stronger relationships. Become self-aware of how you appear to others. Are you playing a role or are you acting like the real you? Pay attention to how you feel. When you act in a certain way, does it feel true to you? Do you feel energized by acting that way? Are you internally motivated to do that action? If so, you are being authentic. If you feel like a fake, like you are trying to be someone you are not, or if you have to be pressured into acting like you care, then you are not being authentic. That creates inner turmoil and mental fatigue. It's not authentic to who you are at your core. You don't have just one identity. You aren't just an athlete, you have other interests, passions, hobbies, etc. Do your best to be authentic to your whole self, not just to individual parts of you.

When: with these drills, I would recommend using them as part of your team rules. You might not include these drills in your practice plan, but I recommend using them as part of your team's code of conduct.

How: See Creating an effective team culture section

What: Communication Drills

COMMUNICATION DRILLS

1. Listening Drill - practice this with a parent or friend. Make sure they know what you are doing, otherwise it could be awkward. Ask a parent or friend to tell you something about their day or an upcoming event. Your task is to listen only! Listen without trying to interrupt or interject. This is a mindfulness practice and a connection opportunity. As you listen, keep your mind focused on the speaker and pay attention to what they are sharing.

2. **Coaching Drill—The next time you are receiving feedback/instruction from a coach, pay attention to your body language. Are you making eye contact? Is your body reacting? (muscle tension, heart rate) Has your posture changed? (head shoulders slumped, head up and listening) What are you thinking about? Are you listening or are you planning a response? Are you paying attention with the mindset that feedback is helpful, even if the feedback is uncomfortable to hear? The goal is to be present so that you can grow from the experience. If you find your mind wandering, focus on taking a deep breath, shifting your posture, and trying not to make excuses.**

3. Communication Drill—If you need to have an uncomfortable conversation, take some time to plan what you want to say. Clarifying what you want to say and how you want to say it can be difficult. Clarify the actual issue you want to bring up. How can you describe it without exaggeration? How can you express your concerns or emotions about the issue in a way that doesn't attack the other person? Say things like when (blank) happened, it made me feel (blank) instead of you made me mad. Taking the time to plan out what you want to say helps you feel more confident. It will also help you be concise and to the point.

When: Anytime you are teaching, coaching, providing feedback to the team or an individual player.

How: The overall intent of this drill is to help athletes be more accepting of the coaching they receive from you. It is important to remember that you play a role in their overall receptiveness. People won't listen to your feedback if you're not good at it and don't follow the BUILD chapter practices.

Coaches should create a safe environment where players can ask questions and make mistakes without fear of being belittled or punished. If psychological safety is not present, it severely hinders an athlete's ability to learn and grow. As a coach, your best bet to create coachable athletes is to make sure your team culture is psychologically safe.

Also, incorporate this drill into your team code of conduct, as I recommend. Set guidelines for athletes on how to receive feedback, including body language, eye contact, and avoiding excuses. If you see and of the body language that shows a player has lost receptiveness, bring it to their attention. Pause the feedback and make sure they are in a headspace to listen again.

What: Critical Self-Talk Drills

CRITICAL SELF-TALK DRILLS

1. **I Can't Drill:** If you're struggling to achieve something and your thoughts have turned unhelpful, then try adding the word yet, to the end of the thought. For example, if you are struggling to learn a specific technique in your sport and you have problems during the drills, you might think, I'm just not good at this, or I can't do this. If you put a yet to the end of the thought, I'm not good at this yet or I can't do this yet, it changes the dynamics of the statement. This "yet" acknowledges the reality of your current skill level but also allows you to remember that you can and will get better if you keep putting in the work. It keeps your thoughts focused on what's possible, even if your current state is not where you want to be. This is also a good time to ask for help from someone who can provide encouragement or instruction to get where you want to be.

2. **Best Friend Drill:** Another way to change your self-talk to be more effective is to ask, Would you say that to your best friend? If you were talking to your best friend the same way you are talking to yourself, would they still be your friend? To change your thinking, ask yourself, what would I say to my best friend if they were dealing with the same thing? How would I help them? And then fill your brain with those thoughts instead of the negative ones you were having.

3. **Self-Praise Drill:** When you've had a long day of hard work/training, you can look in the mirror and say you worked hard today. Great job. Talking to yourself in the mirror may seem strange or uncomfortable, but it is often helpful. Try saying nice things to yourself in the mirror once a day for a continuous period (start with one week) and pay attention to any changes you experience in your thinking. You'll notice that your self-talk gets nicer and more productive throughout the rest of your day, and you are kinder to yourself.

When: These drills are all great for moments when you see a player get down on themselves, hang their head, slump their shoulders. Anytime you think their self-talk has turned negative. Anytime they verbalize things like "I'm no good at this" or "I can't".

How:

1. I can't drill- this one is pretty simple. Respond to athletes' "I can't" with "YET" (remember the Growth Mindset we discussed in BUILD). Emphasize that lack of current skill doesn't mean lack of future potential. Reinforce the growth mindset and remind them to keep trying.

2. Best Friend Drill- you will treat this one similar to the last. Whenever athletes have negative thoughts, ask them if they would say the same thing to their best friend? Help them have productive and purposeful thoughts that focus on possibilities.

3. Self-Praise Drill - This one you can have a bit of fun with. I would consider making it a game, especially if your athletes struggle to maintain an effective mindset. While at practice, set a time limit (5 -10 minutes) and create the rules that the only thinking allowed to come out of their mouths is self-praise or praise of a teammate. Prohibit criticism from being voiced during the time limit. You have to follow the rules too!!! Always find something to praise during team drills. Obviously, you can't do this 24/7. Correction is necessary at some point, just not in this drill! Create some sort of silly penalty for people if they get caught saying something negative (dizzy bat run to first, sing Itsy-Bitsy spider, do a cartwheel). The goal is to be playful, but bring home the point that athletes need to be kinder to themselves. This also forces them to focus more on the positives instead of the negatives, which fight the negativity bias.

What: Self-Compassion Drills

SELF-COMPASSION DRILLS

1. **Write yourself a friendly note.** The note doesn't have to be long, but it can be. Start with just two or three sentences. Write something encouraging, like, I am glad you exist, and I am proud of the work you do. You can give yourself the words that will help you feel more confident.

2. **Spend an hour outside.** Get some fresh air and mindfulness while you spend time at a local park, in the forest, or at the beach. Being in the open air can offer a new sense of calm.

3. **Turn off your phone and pay attention to yourself.** Take a break from social media, texts, and other notifications that take you out of the present moment. By truly immersing yourself in your own time, you'll build a stronger connection to yourself. If this time feels uncomfortable, use it to say productive things to yourself.

4. **Write it out. Keep a journal or notebook for positive, encouraging thoughts about yourself. Write out some critical self-talk phrases and then come up with counter or balancing thoughts that work for you. (see resource section for journal options)**

When: Most of these drills are for individual athletes to use outside of sport. If you can remind or reinforce the tools, then that's a great option. Number 4 makes a great game. Athletes can practice battling negative thoughts beforehand. This helps them feel prepared to do it in pressure situations.

How: Have your team partner up. Each partner describes a moment in the recent past when they had some negative self-talk. They share with their partner a specific moment, like when they struck out or gave up a double. Then each partner takes turns saying a counterproductive thought for that event to their partner. And they have to fight back and create a more productive thought in response.

For clarity sake, I'm going to create 2 fictitious athletes. Here, Susie and Erin are working together. Susie tells Erin about her recent and vivid time when she was having self-critical / counterproductive thoughts. Susie says "last week when I walked the bases loaded then gave up a double, I really started getting negative. I blamed myself for everything that went wrong."

Erin would then provide a specific self-critical thought that Susie might have in that situation. Make sure it's phrased as if Susie was saying it to herself. For example, Erin might say, "I am absolute crap today. I can't do anything right." Susie then has to fight this specific thought by being more productive. She could say, "Yes, I messed up, but my teammates have my back and I know we can get back in this game. Just focus on hitting my spots and let's get out of this inning."

This process would continue until Susie has fought back against a handful (4-6) of thoughts. Then Erin would repeat the process with her situation. Both athletes are getting practice fighting back against negative self-talk in real time. Wait for both athletes to finish, then discuss their performance.

What: How to set S.M.A.R.T. short-term goals

SET SMART SHORT-TERM GOALS

1. **Make your goal specific.** For example, instead of, I want to get more hits or I want to get faster, you can use, I want to increase my batting average to .350 or I want to decrease my split time by 10 seconds. When goals are vague, it's really difficult to determine if you actually succeeded. A short-term goal that is not specific is not helpful in achieving your long-term goal.

2. **Set measurable goals.** I want to get better or I want to be a good hitter is not a measurable goal. My batting average will increase by 25 points or I will decrease my strikeouts by (% or specific number per season or per at bat) is. Ensure that you have some sort of metric to help you determine whether you've met the goal.

3. **Set action-oriented goals.** Focus on what you want to happen versus what you don't want to do. If I tell you don't think about a pink elephant, what happens? Our brains don't have a mental picture for don't or not doing something. For example, if you stay up too late playing video games and it's affecting your performance, using the goal of don't play video games is not an action. Instead, phrase your goal as the replacement behavior or action you will take instead. I will go to bed at 10:30. Instead of don't strike out use hit well with 2 strikes or don't waste time at practice use stay focused and work hard. Phrasing your goal as an action you can take makes it easier to accomplish.

4. **Setting realistic goals is important as well.** I will bench press 400 pounds, may be a realistic goal for some. But if you are a young athlete weighing 120 pounds. It is probably not. Your goals must have some stretch or challenge in them, to move you forward and help you grow, but they need to be possible for you in your current state or level of ability. As you improve, increase the challenge.

5. **Setting time bound goals is critical.** An open-ended goal with no time pressure for completion leads to procrastination. I want to lose weight is a dream. I will lose 2 pounds within the next 7 days is a time bound goal. A goal with no due date gets lost on your schedule of priorities.

When: This is a great drill to start at the beginning of a season. Have conversation with each player to help them create a season goal that is meaningful to them. Then help them build SMART goals throughout the season to move towards that goal. I would also highly recommend that you make this part of your pre-practice routine with athletes. Before practice starts, have everyone write or verbalize 1 specific thing they are trying to get better on at practice today. It can be mental or physical. Then have them develop at least one SMART action they will do at practice to work on it.

How: Make goal setting part of your team culture. I would recommend doing a group session in one of your first practices of the year. Between you and the players, define some key outcome goals that the team is working towards. The specific items you come up with will depend on where and what level you coach. You are looking for things like having a certain record, winning a certain tournament, finishing in the top 5 of the league, etc. Having a specific outcome the entire team is working towards helps create unity and cohesion. These goals become the motivation for the season.

However, it's key to remember that many outcomes are outside of your control. Your team could play their absolute best and still lose tough games or miss the playoffs. Keep in mind that you cannot control many outcomes. You can use them as guides and adjust them as the season unfolds.

The important next step is to have your team develop process related goals that would help them achieve the outcome goals. You are looking for things like:

- practicing hard

- getting 1% better very day

- taking it one pitch at a time

- don't lose 2 innings in a row

- every player committing to 30 minutes a week of practice on their own.

You want them to focus on the process of creating the outcomes they want. If you have a returning squad, you can add 1-2 SMART goals that focus on the weaknesses from the previous year.

The process should follow the feedback principles from BUILD that involve players in goal creation. This creates more buy-in and commitment to the process because they are creating it.

After setting team goals, ask players to set their own individual goals to help the team. Have players focus on progress over perfection. Players should share their ideas in small groups at the next practice. Perhaps even have players help each other refine the goals using the SMART principles. Again, set conditions. Don't judge anyone's goals as everyone has their own journey. For example, if you work with a recreational team and have a player whose goal is to get a bunt down in a game before the end of the season. Maybe they haven't learned that well, or they fear getting hit by the ball and want to get better at bunting. If many players already possess the skill, mocking the aspiring bunter for her "silly goal" would be unfair and pretty awful.

Try to create time to have each player share their goals with you individually so that you can also advise and assist them in making progress. They might be unsure of the right drills for improving their bunting. This is where you could add your help. There are a few ways to do this.

1. Have players submit their goals in writing to you. Goals in writing save time but lack discussion and feedback. You could, however, take notes on their goals and review it with them at a later practice to create the dialogue.

2. Create a station at practice in which every player has to cycle through you, as the goal setting station for the day. 5 minutes per player depending on the size of your team should be reasonable. You will, of course, need help from other parents/coaches to run other stations while you do this.

3. Have everyone share their goal out loud with the team. This option has multiple benefits. Everyone can help keep each other accountable. It's an opportunity for you to help shape the goals for everyone to hear so that they might make some corrections on their goals. This option will pair nicely with the "Accountablilibuddy" system that I talk about later.

*Side note: As a coach, you should also develop personal goals to help the team reach its goals. Share these with your team. They can include game management, the way you run practice, the quality of your feedback, etc. Share and model the process for your team.

What: Discover Your Values Drill

DISCOVER YOUR VALUES DRILL

Follow this process to determine your values:

1. Begin by making a list of things you value (at least 10 things). Write them as a full sentence (Family should come first) vs just a word (Family). Think about how you try to live your life. What principles do you hold? How do you think you should act? How should people treat others or handle problems? What values do your parents, coaches, and mentors think are important? Create your list to help you figure out what values matter to you.

2. Next, shorten that list to 3 - 6 values that are core or central to how you live your life (or want to) and begin visualizing them in your daily life.

3. Write each value down and put them somewhere where you see them each day (your mirror, desk, bedroom door or wall, gear bag).

4. Refer to your values often, and check-in with yourself to see if you're living up to them. If you stray, refocus onto your values without judgment or negative self-talk.

5. Setting your values helps during times of stress, because they give you a guideline for how you would like to live. Before you make any big decisions, pause in a moment of mindfulness and consult your values. They often offer a stronger perspective to make the best decision possible in any situation.

When: In this case, I would recommend doing this exercise as a team. It is a great team building exercise to help everyone get on the same page and create an effective team culture.

How: See Team Culture Section for specific details

What: Deliberate Breathing Drills

DELIBERATE BREATHING DRILLS

1. Deliberate breathing is something you should practice regularly in order to train you body to engage the calming response. Build breath practice into you day-to-day routine. Pick a time and place that you will devote 2-3 minutes practice your deliberate breathing. Focus on breathing low and slow. Pay with the different rhythms above to discover which works best for you.

2. To practice using your deliberate breath under stressful conditions spend one minute getting your heart rate up with some form of exercise (jumping jacks, run in place, burpees). The exercise mimics what it feels like to be nervous in a big moment. When the minute is over start taking slow deliberate breaths. The goal is to get your heart rate back down as quickly as possible. Your eventual goal top get your heart rate back under control should be about 2-3 breathes.

When: It is possible to build both drills into your practice routine. The first drill (2-3 minute breathing) would be best during breaks and in transition between drills. You can incorporate the second drill into a specific practice routine for the best results.

How:

1. This is pretty simple: make breathing part of your water breaks. Instruct players to sit on the bench and breathe low and slow into their abdomen. Set a timer for 1-3 minutes. Once the breathing is done, athletes can get water, change gear for the next drill, and chitchat a bit until the break is over.

2. I recommend doing this drill as designed first. Pick a drill that requires focus and deliberate execution. Ideas might include:

- having hitters bunt to a specific location

- fielders to hit a specific target with a throw

- pitchers hitting a specific target (pitch outs)

- reaction drills that require a player to adjust on the fly to bad hops

- 2-2 count at scrimmage at bats with runners on, etc.

You are looking for a drill that would be difficult to execute well if the athlete cannot control their physiology or heart rate.

Have the player conduct 60 seconds of heart rate elevating exercise (sprint, jumping jacks, burpees) then step into the drill. Complete the exercise just before starting the task. They should NOT have a break that allows their heart rate to return to normal. Let athletes know that the goal of the drill is to practice controlling their heart rate and physiology. Yes, they want to perform well in the drill, but that is a secondary focus.

It is normal that athletes cannot return their heart rate back to baseline right away. You could have athletes measure their heart rate by putting two fingers on a pulse (neck or wrist) to gauge whether their breathing is working. The goal is to calm down enough to be functional. They don't have to be 100% calm. It's likely they would rarely be that way in an actual game. It is normal to be nervous in big moments. With this drill, athletes can figure out when their nerves are unproductive and how to regulate their heart rate.

What: Refocus Drills

REFOCUS DRILLS

1. You can practice while doing any sport related task or even your homework. Build your AIR plan before you start. Then set a timer for 5 minutes. During that time anytime you get distracted use your planned AIR technique. You can even pre-plan some distractions have a parent or friend purposely try to distract you during that 5 minutes.
2. Trash talk competition. Pick a sport specific drill that you can do with a parent or friend. Pick a drill that has some sort of metric or measurement of how well you are doing it. (Hitting balls off of a tee to a specific location in the cage, making free throws, spot passing, taking shots on goal). You and your friend/parent should perform the drill once to determine your baseline score. Then during your second attempt have your friend trash-talk you or try to distract you in any way they want, that doesn't prevent you from actually performing the drill (they can't steal the ball or block the goal). You will have to use the AIR technique to stay focused or to fight back against counterproductive thoughts. The fun part is that you will switch places with your friend/parent. Whoever performs closest to their baseline score on the second attempt wins the game. This is fun because even if you have different skill levels you are actually trying to beat or match your own previous score not the other person's score.

When: This is a great drill to build into practice as an opportunity to have fun, build positive emotion and have a bit of good natured competition.

How: Make sure you teach the AIR technique to your players before doing this drill.

Choose a task that can be scored easily since the drill is easy to understand. Have players buddy up and everybody do the drill without distraction to get their base score. Once baseline scores are obtained, partners can engage in trash talking or distracting shenanigans. Be sure to set clear ground rules on what counts as trash talking. Anything that distracts or frustrates the partner doing the task. But it should not be mean-spirited or demeaning. And remember that the partner cannot interfere with the ability to complete the task. As long as they met these basic guidelines, everything else is fair game at this point. They can dance, sing, catcall, yell, whatever they want to distract their partner.

You could even turn this into a Last Man Standing type of elimination competition. Create a bracket. After one partner wins beating their own baseline score, they now partner up with a winner from a fresh pair and play again. Winners keep playing winners until there is one ultimate victor. If you would like to amp it up, have the losers become the winners' entourage. All losing partners must follow whoever they lost too. They can engage in trash talk with their winner in upcoming competitions. In the final round, the remaining winners will receive help from teammates to distract their opponents. This gets loud, rowdy, and fun. Just remember to reiterate the rules.

*It's also important to remember that the goal is for individual players to be competing against their OWN baseline. So even if they are playing against a much more skilled athlete, whoever is closest to their baseline score or beats their baseline score by the most wins.

**You might have to make sure that athletes don't sandbag their baseline score. Which means they should not purposely score low or poorly on their baseline attempt. You know the skill level of your players. If it looks like someone scored way below their normal, make them re-establish their baseline.

CHAPTER 7: INCORPORATING MENTAL SKILLS DRILLS INTO GAMES

I used my background as an athlete and experience in mental skills training to create the Personal Performance Plan (PPP). The PPP is a framework for incorporating all the tools and skills that I've taught in Confident, Calm and Clutch and this Coach's Companion. It provides you structure of when and where to help your athletes use and apply the skills.

When athletes can apply the skills and drills in Confident, Calm and Clutch, they can improve their performance and be more mentally tough while doing it.

I do not mean the Personal Performance Plan framework to be a set of strict rules. They are best practices based on my experience as a player, as a teacher of this material, and supported by the research in sports psychology. The framework makes it easier to apply mental toughness tools in real time when it matters.

This structure will help you better advise and coach your athletes when and how to use specific strategies in a game. This framework assumes that you have taught these skills prior to the game. You are now shifting the focus from Discover and Build to Apply.

I've given you a lot of tools and skills to help your athletes perform better, but it can feel overwhelming not knowing when to use what. Four logical time frames exist in every performance: before, right before, during, and after. Athletes can use the PPP framework to create their own plan to perform at their best.

The basic things that your athletes are trying to control at all times is their mind-body connection. Where is their **attention**, what's happening in their **body** (emotions and physiology), and how is their **confidence**? I call these the ABCs of performance. If your athlete's ABCs are in a productive place, they will set conditions for success.

By teaching your athletes to DISCOVER, they should have a solid understanding of where their ABC's need to be for success. The PPP helps them be deliberate before, during, and after a game in managing their ABCs. The framework helps athletes choose the skills they need to perform well, even though each athlete may need a unique approach to their ABCs.

Let's dive into the structure. Remember, these are guidelines, not hard and fast rules.

Before	Right Before	During	After
When:_____	When:_____	When:_____	When:_____
What's my goal?	Write out your Pre-performance routine. Include all relevant ABC's.	What can I control?	Get Curious:
Process Goals (2-3):		Refocus plan:	Recovery/transition plan:
3 Good things for confidence:		Indicators that I need to breathe:	Goal for next game:
Take time to mentally rehearse yourself achieving your goals.			

Personal Performance Plan Performance: _____

Use this plan to manage the ABC's of Performance: Attention, Body, Confidence

Valahun Coaching

Before Phase: Consider the before phase to be like the training phase. The goal of this phase is to prepare for a specific game or opponent. It could last weeks, days, or hours. It depends on the context of your game schedule. To establish a timeframe for explanation, assume today is Monday and you have a game on Saturday. The period before the game is your BEFORE phase. In this case, Monday through Friday.

Confident, Calm, and Clutch skills are essential for preparing and performing well in this phase. Things like:

- Goal setting - understanding what you're trying to accomplish in this game on Saturday. What's the game plan? Identify two to three steps (SMART goals) that make sure you are actually ready to play.

- Three Good Things Exercise- to reflect on successes and build confidence leading up the game.

- Mindfulness tools

- Get Curious Drill

This stage is for getting ready to perform. Whichever tools help you get the most out of practice, use them. Your athletes may choose to use other tools, but these are the things that research and my experience suggests works best in this stage.

Right Before Phase: The right before phase is game day (Saturday). When players start their pre-performance routine. The goal of this phase is to prime and ready your athletes to perform. The pre-performance routine can range from 5 minutes to 1-2 hours, depending on several factors. As soon as you begin your pre-game routine as a team, you have definitely entered the Right Before phase.

The pre-performance routine is simple. It involves any of the tools that help athletes get their attention, body and confidence ready to play. You will have team warm-ups to give it structure, but you should remind your players to add-in the individual tools they need.

This may include:

- Critical Self-Talk Drills

- Self-Compassion Drills

- Deliberate Breathing

- Mindfulness Drills

I recommend these tools for preparing to perform, although their use may vary by person. Athletes need a deliberate process (physical and mental) to get ready to play. Then you transition into performing.

During Phase: This is the actual game itself. Saturday when the umpire says "play ball!" The goal of this phase is to focus on executing and trusting your skills. You want to keep it simple and play. You want your athletes to be in a mindful, alert, and focused state. The aim is to keep athletes focused on what they can control and to remain confident.

The tools best suited for this phase are:

- Refocus techniques (AIR or Grounding)

- Deliberate Breathing

- Reframing Drill

- Critical Self-Talk Drills

During a game there are several mini-moments of right before/during that players cycle through. For example, a pre-performance routine for an at bat or between innings shifting from offense and defense. Softball and baseball games offer natural pauses to shift between smaller before and during moments. But the overall during phase is game time. Your athletes are performing.

After Phase: To excel, reflect and get curious after finishing the game. Re-enter discover mode to analyze what worked, what didn't, and the strategic insights gained about the team. This is the after phase.

The goal is to learn, grow, gain confidence, assess game plans, and develop new goals for future games. In particular, when there are multiple games in a day. The other intent of this phase is to rest, recover, and reset. You may have more games to play that day and need to recoup energy.

Skills that will help this phase are:

- Get Curious Drill

- Reframe Drill

- Review and assess Goals

- Three Good Things Activity - boosts confidence by focusing on what went right.

- Deliberate Breathing

The intent is to reflect non-judgmentally and allow athletes to discover. The after phase time-frame may vary if you have another game. If you have back-to-back games, make sure you balance reflection with recovery.

Use the things that worked for your team to build confidence for the next game. And develop a plan to fix or tweak what didn't work. I would highly recommend you take notes and record any valuable insights and data to help the team/players in the future. Allow time for athletes to reflect on their individual and team performance.

This phase's lessons should guide the next game's Before phase. The Personal Performance Plan is a very cyclical process. It's a very simple strategy or framework for how to apply the Confident, Calm and Clutch skills.

Athletes can use a PPP to prepare for their opponents. Athletes are devising a literal plan for controlling what they can control to maximize performance. They are figuring out how they will remain Confident, Calm and Clutch during the game. By thinking about it ahead of time and jotting down some notes, it helps athletes solidify their plan and allows them to be more deliberate.

Developing a Personal Performance Plan doesn't mean you're always going to be successful. Be your best by controlling what you can and eliminating barriers. It won't guarantee success. Athletes make mistakes, they're human. But if you use this framework, you're setting conditions to be more successful.

Encourage athletes to pick one performance to start with. Anything goes: tournament, game, or moment. Using the structure of PPP (see worksheet), have them develop a plan that builds confidence, helps them stay calm and allows them to be clutch in key moments. Use time before or after practice to help athletes through the process.

This Personal Performance Plan process is most useful for athletes who have learned various mental skills drills. It's an easy way for athletes inexperienced with mental skills to prepare for games. You are asking your athletes to be proactive and deliberate about preparing for games. That will never be a bad thing. But having skills to manage their mind, body and emotions, is more valuable.

See Resources page at the end of this book for a Printable PPP Worksheet

Chapter 8: Journaling

Why Should Your Athletes Keep a Journal?

Journaling proves to be a powerful tool that benefits many aspects of life, such as making sense of a complicated day or tracking personal growth. And the world of sports is no exception. In this chapter, we'll discuss the power of journaling to help teen athletes keep track of their results and build confidence in their abilities. I will explain why coaches should encourage athletes to use a journal, give tips, and introduce my special journal for better results.

Now I know many people hear the word journaling and say, "Eh that's not for me, I don't want to write a bunch of fluffy stuff in a diary." So what do I mean actually by journaling?

Journaling is simply the act of recording what you did and how it went. Think of it as **record keeping, note taking, list making, data collection**. If you were "journaling" about your strength training workouts, you would want to keep track of which lifts you did, reps, weights, etc and how it went in order to assess your progress and be able to guide your next workout. If last week you did the bench press for 3 sets of 10 reps at 100 lbs, this week you would be able to make adjustments to either the sets, reps or weight based on what you are trying to accomplish. But if you never journaled or kept a record of what you did and how it went, you would have no idea what to do the following week to improve your strength. Record keeping is an essential element of training and development.

You can choose to have your athletes journal or record keep in any way that works for them. Any form of paper/pencil combination will work but they can use word documents, notes on their phone, voice memos. The method is less important than ensuring they reflect on the right things to help them grow and thrive. One of your important tasks as a coach is to help athletes overcome any barriers they have to journaling / record keeping. If an athlete is reluctant to journal then simple ask them to make notes or track what they did. The word journaling bothers some people, so use a word that doesn't prevent them from keeping good records of their activities, thoughts and outcomes.

The Importance of Journaling for Athletes

Journaling isn't just about putting pen to paper. The process of self-reflection helps athletes improve by identifying their strengths and weaknesses. Keeping track of progress can help athletes enhance motivation and achieve their goals.

Processing Games and Practice Results

One major benefit of journaling is that it allows athletes to process the results of their games and practices. By doing so, they can learn from their experiences and adopt strategies to improve their performance. By journaling, athletes can identify behavior patterns that help or hinder their performance and improve their skills. Essentially, all of the work you do in the **Discover** process has somewhere to go!

Tracking Growth and Development

Journaling can serve as concrete proof of an athlete's growth and development. Keeping track of their achievements and setbacks helps them review their progress and identify trends. Coaches and athletes can use this data to identify areas of improvement and develop strategies to achieve them.

Building Confidence

Keeping a journal can help fuel an athlete's confidence. Documenting their journey can remind athletes of how far they've come and the progress they've made. Celebrating small achievements is important for building self-esteem and resilience.

Tips for Effective Athlete Journaling

1. **Consistency**: Encourage your athletes to write in their journal regularly, whether it's daily, weekly, or after every practice/game.

2. **Honesty**: Athletes should be truthful about their feelings and thoughts when journaling. This will provide valuable insights into their mindset. They should also be honest about the quality of their effort, energy, and performance.

3. **Goals**: Help your athletes set specific, measurable, action-oriented, relevant, and time-bound (SMART) goals to improve.

4. **Review**: Regularly review the journal entries with your athletes to discuss their progress and provide guidance.

5. **Reflection:** Encourage athletes to look for patterns in their journal entries that can guide their future actions.

As a coach, using journaling on your team helps athletes understand their progress and build confidence, leading to a growth mindset that benefits both their athletic careers and lives. You can start by having athletes bring a simple notebook to practice. Or you can order the Confident, Calm and Clutch Journal for your team (see resources page). Make journaling a priority and watch your athletes flourish in their sport.

And as with everything else in this guide, practice what you preach. Make sure you engage in your own journaling practice as a coach. Engage in the Discover, Build, Apply method on your own to better master the process and guide your own growth and development.

Chapter 9: Effective Team Culture

"As a leader, your attitude has a powerful impact on others. Whether that impact is positive or negative depends on the choices you make. You have an obligation to develop a positive attitude, one that inspires the people around you to achieve the impossible." -Lou Holtz

"Leaders create culture. Culture drives behavior. Behavior produces results." - Coach Urban Meyer

What is team culture, and why should you work hard to create one? Well, I think the quote above states it pretty well. Team culture is essential to results. But it's also essential to creating an environment that helps athletes grow and thrive. It's difficult to help athletes build their athletic skills and mental toughness without an effective team culture that embodies the tenants of trust, psychological safety, fun, commitment and growth.

Creating an effective team culture includes the parents (if relevant) of your team. Without parent support for the team's expectations, problems will persist. If you are working with youth athletes, then managing parents is a major aspect of coaching. Based on my and my coaching friends' experience, this can be the hardest part. Parents spend more time with their kids than you do. If you have not gotten their buy-in for the culture that you expect on your team, that will only make your life harder.

Do you ever wonder why some organizations are consistently successful, and others are not? Is there some magic set of values that attracts people to elite organizations and repels them from bad ones? I believe the answer is yes. I believe that there are three keys to getting your athletes to buy in to your vision for your team.

What Players Need to Thrive on Your Team

1. Your players must believe that your vision is a worthy of their personal investment.

2. Your players must believe that they are good at what they do and can help the vision manifest successfully.

3. Your athletes must believe that you understand them, appreciate them, and respect them.

How to build a foundation for your culture

1. Create a set of core values they can believe in.

2. Set a team goal(s) they can buy in to with an accompanying motto or slogan.

3. Create an environment where everyone has a role and everyone understands all roles are critical to team success.

How to execute your vision for your team

So once you have built this template for success, you are all done, right? Not exactly. There are actually three more things you need to do.

1. You must recruit players who align with your vision and agree to put the team first.

2. You must get rid of players and/or parents who undermine your core values and your goals.

3. You must model the behavior you expect from your team at all times.

Example: Below is a story of my 10U Batbuster team. I share this story because the coach was able to utilize the principles above. I was the youngest player on the team the previous year and when everyone moved up to 12U my dad volunteered to coach the 10U team. He essentially had to create a whole new team. He wanted to create a specific culture that would help me learn and grow as a player and create a good competitive team.

Here are the core values my dad worked with the team to develop.

Core Values:

1. Do the right thing even when you don't feel like it and no-one is watching.

2. Treat other people with the respect they deserve.

3. Strive for excellence at all times and in all things

Our team goal was: To Compete Hard in Every Game We Played Regardless of the Score

Our Motto was: Play Hard, Have Fun, No Mercy

Our Aspiration was to win the National Championship Tournament in Broken Arrow, Oklahoma

That team consisted of 13 nine- and ten-year-old athletes from Southern California. We played virtually every weekend from September through August, culminating in the National Championship Tournament in August. Our record for the year was 110 wins and 6 losses, with 5 of those losses coming to 12 & under teams, we played in invitational tournaments when we played up an age bracket.

I did not learn until just recently (when I started writing this book) all that my dad did to keep that team on track over the course of the season. There were players upset with lack of playtime. There were parents upset with their daughter's role. There were players who couldn't afford to play on the team. And there were times when some parents thought we should back off on our training and intensity. I was never aware of this as a kid. Because my dad made sure that these distractions never affected his players.

In fact, it wasn't until just a few years ago that my dad finally told me about an incident that happened at the National Tournament. The 72 team tournament began on Thursday and ended on Sunday. We won our first few games to remain in the winner's bracket on Friday night. We had a big lead in our late game Friday, so dad put one of our reserve outfielders in the game in left field for the final two innings.

He knew this girl would possibly not get a chance to play as the games became more important. He had defined her role as an emergency player who would be available, if needed, off the bench. Dad's promise to her was that he would find a way to get her into a game in the tournament to reward her efforts on behalf of the team.

Unfortunately, another parent whose daughter was also a reserve player, was upset because her daughter had not got to play yet. Dad had cast her daughter's role as a pinch hitter. His deal with the player was that when he had a runner on third and less than two outs, he would bring her in to pinch hit and drive in the run. And that situation had not yet occurred in our previous games.

One parent got upset. Then two parents started pushing back. Groups of parents then chose sides. Then everyone started grousing at each other. And this was in the parking lot as my teammates and I were being transported back to the hotel for dinner, so we missed it. Because dad was meeting with the tournament officials, he didn't see most of this until he was on his way to the parking lot. By the time he got there, it was a pretty vocal feud.

Question Break

Take a minute and think about what you would do to resolve this situation.

Are you ready to see what he did?

Back to the story

Dad called a closed door meeting. He had Mom (aka amazing Champion Support Team member) take us girls to dinner and told all the parents to meet him in the conference room at the hotel.

When all the parents arrived, he began:

"I want to remind you of the core values you agreed to as a member of this team."

1. Do the right thing even when you don't feel like it and no-one is watching.

2. Treat other people with the respect they deserve.

3. Strive for excellence at all times and in all things

"I want to remind you of our goals and aspirations."

Our team goal was: To Compete Hard in Every Game We Played Regardless of the Score

Our Motto was: Play Hard, Have Fun, No Mercy

Our Aspiration was to win the National Championship Tournament in Broken Arrow, Oklahoma

He explained the plan he had developed for each player and why it was consistent with our values, goals and aspirations.

He then did something powerful. He pulled out his check book. (Yeah paper checks. Do you remember those?)

And he said:

Our daughters have the opportunity to do something very special. They are in a position to earn a National Championship. There is no guarantee they will ever have this opportunity again. I expect one of two things from you. Either you show up to the games and cheer enthusiastically for every child on the team, or you can get on a plane and go home. I will write you a check for the cost of changing your ticket. But I will not allow you to undermine the goals this team has set. Your feelings do not matter to me. Your daughter has worked her ass off to be here and she deserves the chance to complete our mission. I do not care if you like each other. I do not care if you like me. What I do care about is that you do not sabotage this team.

Then he said: Your daughters and I are here to win. Don't get in our way. And left the meeting.

So what happened? Everyone showed up at the games and behaved. We got into a tough battle late Saturday night with the local favorite team and ended up losing a close game. This was our only loss all year to a 10U team. We had to come back Sunday morning and win the losers bracket final for the right to play the winner. Then we had to beat them twice to win the tournament.

The elements were against us. It was hot and muggy, with a heat index of 110.

The crowd was against us. The team we were playing was the hometown Broken Arrow Thunderbirds.

We had trained to stay focused. We had trained to play hard no matter what. At our team meeting on Sunday morning, we agreed to go out and "Kick some Bird Butt!" We loved close games. We loved the pressure.

So what happened?

We made it to the championship game and had to use every player on the roster to persevere and win the tournament. Our pinch hitter got six chances to drive in runs and did it every time. When the final out was recorded, we were exhausted, but had achieved the National Title.

So what is the moral of this story? A coach needs to set the values, vision and goals for the team. The team needs to attract and retain players that commit to the vision. And when it matters most, the coach has to step up and not let anything or anyone undermine that vision.

Leadership is why some teams thrive, and others don't. Leaders lead, whiners whine, Losers lose. Winners compete. Even if they lose the game, they win respect.

What is Culture?

Culture = Attitudes + Behaviors.

"It includes the values, beliefs, behaviors, artifacts, and reward systems that influence people's behavior on a day-to-day basis."–Deloitte

This is the team/ organization's "way of doing things." Some say, "it's how we do things around here." All teams have a culture, by default or by design. People, good or bad convey culture. Ensure that your team culture is intentional and not left up to chance.

Elite organizations do not happen by accident, but by deliberate intention. Research characterizes truly effective teams by:

- a team philosophy and

- an atmosphere that allows all members to share in creating group goals and objectives;

- they can speak openly about issues which affect them,

- the ability to deal with conflict openly and constructively.

There are many ways to create an effective team culture. Here are four basic ways to help you set conditions for success.

1. **Code of Conduct**

2. **Define the character and values that are important to your team**

3. **Create a shared vision / goal**

4. **Create accountability**

Code of Conduct

A good code of conduct is important for sports teams, but the traditional method of making them is uninspiring. You cannot build trust and a healthy team culture on general phrases like "do the right thing" and "treat others with respect". In this chapter, you'll learn a new way to create a code of conduct that encourages responsibility, psychological safety, and success.

Boosting Team Culture:

You can't have a successful team without a strong culture. A code of conduct should help to foster it, not hinder it. You build culture on shared values and behaviors that everyone on the team must uphold. Implementing a code of conduct can help communicate these values consistently to athletes, coaches, and parents. Instead of handing out a 10-page document no one bothers to read, use storytelling to illustrate the importance of these values to your team. This way, your team will be more likely to embrace the spirit of your code of conduct, rather than simply following a rigid set of rules.

Accountability, not Punitive Measures:

Too often, people who create codes of conduct focus on punishing athletes, coaches, or parents who do something wrong. This approach works in the short-term, but it can breed resentment and mistrust. A good code of conduct prioritizes accountability over punishment. Coaches and parents need to hold athletes accountable for their actions and teach them to be responsible. When they fall short, it's not about punishment, but about trying to help them get back on track.

Support Psychological Safety:

Psychological safety is key to any team's success. Athletes, coaches, and parents can speak freely without fear of punishment, demeaning behavior or ridicule. Making psychological safety a priority in a code of conduct improves communication and builds trust among team members. If you set clear expectations and encourage open dialogue, your team will feel supported and understood.

Encourages Self-Awareness:

A good code of conduct should encourage athletes, coaches, and parents to be self-aware. They should know the impact they have on others and the reputation they're building for themselves. Self-awareness in a team leads to empathy, better communication, and stronger relationships.

Sets the Tone for Success:

Finally, your code of conduct should set the tone for success. It should inspire athletes to strive for excellence on and off the field. If athletes understand their actions off the field affect the team, they're more likely to act in ways that benefit everyone. A conduct code can inspire athletes to their full potential.

Creating a code of conduct for your team is not just about ticking boxes to ensure everyone is on the same page. It's about setting a standard that inspires your athletes to be their best selves, as both team members and individuals. Building a team culture of openness, accountability, and psychological safety can lead to success on and off the field.

In the next section, I provide a specific exercise that will help your team craft a meaningful code of conduct. Remember that it's not about being boring or formulaic, it's about setting your team up for success, and the best way to do that is to involve them.

Creating a shared vision and defining your values

During the team-building process, it is essential that coaches understand that each team's "formula for success" is unique to that team. Teams can be composed with players from all over the United States (depending on the level at which you coach), region, county, etc who often have completely different backgrounds. Embrace diversity when building a team. Coaches should answer these questions:

What makes each individual unique?

How does this feed into what makes the team unique?

What common vision will the entire team unite behind?

In order to get the most buy-in, involve the entire team. This could include the parents if it makes sense. Or just have the coaches and athletes develop it, then inform the parents of culture/code the team developed.

Coaches need to give up their individual goals for the team's goals. Teams work harder to achieve goals they helped create. Including athletes at every level in the process creates ownership. It speeds up assigning responsibility for each portion of the team's creed, vision, or goal-plan.

Most times, coaches will find that their athletes will set higher goals than the coaches do. Young passionate athletes often have less understanding of their supposed "constraints" which enables them to dream big.

When athletes play a part in establishing the direction of a team, they have a greater tendency to hold their peers to the same high standard. Involving athletes in the culture building process equates to better overall team discipline. Which makes a noticeable difference during training and practice. Every athlete's input is valuable, whether they're a starter, role player, or bench warmer. This leads to increased involvement and commitment.

You can conduct the next series of steps at the first meeting of the year, first practice or across 3-4 practices at the beginning of the season. I learned this activity while working with the military and it is an amazing process for establishing a shared vision and culture for a team.

You will need some basic supplies like paper, pencils, flip chart or whiteboard, and markers. I highly recommended that you take pictures of everything that gets created, and then, when you have time, type up the results and create a "finished" product. (see sample finished products at the end).

Step 1: Identify traits of great teams and/ or organizations (15-25 min)

Introduce the topic of "Great Teams" and the value of pulling from personal experiences of being on past great teams. A "Great Team" is a team that achieves significant results and has high levels of motivation, engagement, and trust. Giving the group time to reflect individually and take notes on past teams before the smaller group discussion is helpful. You might even ask them to do this part as "homework" before showing up at the meeting/practice.

Split the team into 4-6 small groups (4-5 person groups, to include the coaching staff). Each group should answer these questions about a great team they were involved with. Reflect on a great team you know of (college, professional, etc) if you don't have personal experience of being on one.

Reflection questions: What did that team accomplish? What made that team great? What quality, characteristic, or trait did the team possess to make their success possible?

Each person will share their experience of being on a great team. They should describe what the team achieved, and the most important qualities, characteristics, or traits it possessed. Each group will generate a collective list of characteristics from everyone in the group.

Have some pens, paper, clipboards, etc available for each group to write their answers.

Step 2: Narrow Down the List of Traits (20-30 min)

Staying in the small groups, they should choose the 6-8 essential traits for a great team from the collective list. Make sure you record each group's list of 6-8 traits on a Master List that everyone can see (whiteboard/flip chart).

Keep the team in their small groups. You have the option to mix up the groups for each step. Now, from the Master List, have each of the small groups pick their top two choices for great team traits that would have the greatest positive impact on the team. Let the groups know that there **will** be debate and discussion. This is normal and productive. This dialogue helps players get to know each other and create meaningful conversation. But at some point, each group needs to pick their top two. There doesn't have to be a consensus, just a majority.

Gather the team and ask each group to share their top two traits. Write these traits under "Great Team Traits" on a flip chart or whiteboard. Note and merge the traits that are chosen by more than one group. (e.g. If one group says "Trust", write it once, then put a check mark by it anytime another group also says it)

Step 3: Pick your team traits. (20-30 min)

Next, you will use the traits selected by the entire group to build a Great Team Model for your team. Using the list you've created on the flip chart / whiteboard, narrow it down to the top key traits for the team. You are looking for a handful of traits (4-6). When you narrow down the list, examine the traits closely to identify the ones that can be combined with or used to define others and the ones that are redundant.

Ask about the key qualities required for the team or areas that need improvement from last year's performance.

It is important at this stage to get consensus on the key traits for the team. Ask the group to look at what they have decided. Emphasize the importance of obtaining a consensus, or at least having everyone's opinion heard. Encourage everyone to speak up if they have questions or problems with any of the characteristics, or if there are any critical elements missing.

Step 4: Identify behavioral indicators of key traits (20-30 min)

In this step, you need to create a clear description of the identified characteristics. Don't forget to add the language of any other mentioned characteristics. This improves future accountability.

I recommend breaking the team back down into small groups and assigning each group a key trait. If you have 6 traits, you need 6 groups. The group's job is to give an example of each trait in action (i.e., how would someone know this characteristic was being expressed at practice? In a game?). The group should decide on 2-4 behavioral indicators for each key trait that everyone can agree to.

For example: if the team has chosen "trust each other" ask a key trait. *How would someone know this characteristic was being expressed at practice? In a game?*

That could include behaviors like: When teammates make mistakes, we pick them up with high-fives and encouragement, everyone cheers for everyone on the team, we back up every play no matter what, we trust our teammates to try their best every play, etc.

Small groups will share their key trait descriptions with the larger group. This is when the entire team can provide input to refine the behaviors or add obvious behaviors that are missing.

These behaviors and traits can now become your team's Code of Conduct.

Step 5: What's the Goal? How do we know our season was successful? (15-20 min)

Once you define the team's traits and identity, you can define what success means for your team this year/season.

By working on the values / traits first, you get a better sense of what your athletes care about. Use this to align goals with the team's chosen traits.

Between you and the players, define key outcome goals that the team is working towards. This will depend on the level you coach at. You are looking for things like having a certain record, winning a certain tournament, finishing in the top 5 of the league, etc. You can choose to split the team into small groups and have each group come up with 2 goals. Then share and narrow down the list. Ultimately, you are looking for 1-3 key outcomes. Any more that this is overwhelming.

I would consider just asking: At the end of the season, how will we know we have been successful?

Keep it open, see what they come up with. Some people may focus on outcomes, while others may focus on growth and development. Either are great options for defining success. I would recommend that as a coach, if your team doesn't have a growth and development related goal, you should have one personally. How will you gauge the growth and improvement of your athletes as a coach at season end?

Optional based on time:

Once you define "success," you can instruct the group to create SMART goals for ensuring progress towards the defined success. You are looking for 2-3 SMART goals per outcome goal. Again, you can break the team down into smaller groups to work on each individual outcome goal. There will probably be overlap with the behaviors that the team identified in step 4, which is why it is optional. Ask the group if there are any more behaviors required to achieve our goals, besides the ones listed.

Optional based on time: Decide on a theme for the year / season.

Choose a word or phrase that summarizes the great team traits, goals, and action plans that you have agreed upon. The idea is to create a mantra, slogan, or motto for the year.

If you need help with the Great Teams activity for your team, reach out to me at valerie.alston@valstoncoaching.com

Create Accountability

If players help create the team's values, they are more likely to follow them and hold themselves accountable. However, you can also implement other strategies of accountability.

One suggestion is to create "accountabilibuddies." These can rotate throughout the season so that people are mixing it up. You can assign an accountabilibuddy per game / practice or it can be for a chunk of time that makes sense (weekend, week, etc.). The purpose of an accountabilibuddy is to provide support for each other. You might adjust the role based on the age of your athletes, but some ideas may include:

- Assigned cheerleader

- Help each other stay focused

- Negative thinking inspector (help each other stay productive and positive, especially after mistakes)

- Confidence builder

- Throwing and warm up partners

- Look for signs of worry, doubt, fear

- Effort and attitude checks

- Run or work drills together

- They can give each other feedback on what they did well at the end of the game/practice.

- 3 Good Things exercise buddy

- Buddies can monitor and redirect each other's behavior if it goes against the team core values.

You can assign players to keep coaches accountable for being appropriate in their mindset, feedback, and behavior. This can help every player feel involved and relevant even if they are a bench warmer or role player.

Each player should have a role in every game. This keeps the subs actively involved in helping the team win. Maybe they didn't play, but they still helped the team win.

To increase accountability, athletes can help decide consequences for breaking the code of conduct. Thoroughly understanding that actions have consequences is valuable for young people. By creating and having very clear behavior standards on your team and associated consequences it helps everyone get on the same page. When you involve athletes in creating the accountability system, they have stronger buy-in because they pick consequences that are reasonable and doable by them.

It is important to ensure the consequences are reasonable and appropriate for the age and ability of your team. These consequences should never be demeaning, shaming, or embarrassing. The goal is accountability, not to create fear and anxiety. The aim in all cases is to help the athlete grow and develop by applying consequences, then helping them change behavior in a positive direction. Things like if you don't attend practice (unless previously arranged and communicated), you don't start in the next game. Or if you are late to practice, you run two laps.

You want to create a system that focuses primarily on factors that the athletes have control over (effort, attitude, behavior, speech, etc). Young athletes who can't drive shouldn't face consequences for being late to practice, as it is not something they can control.

Whatever you come up with then needs to be applied fairly and consistently. Depending on the age of your athletes, you might also include them in the decision-making process when applying rules in unique contexts. Let's say you are coaching a high school team and 2-3 of your players break a team rule that would normally require them to sit for at least 1 game. But because of injuries, you need these players to ensure you have 9 healthy players for the game. Request the team's opinion. Should they stick to the team rules and potentially forfeit the game, or adjust the consequence in this specific case and allow the offending players to play in the game?

Letting the athletes solve problems by communicating rules and dilemmas allows them to take ownership and learn valuable life skills. However, you can still make the final decision.

Taking these steps to create and sustain an effective team culture will make your job as a coach much easier in the long run. Culture drives behavior. If you can set up an effective team culture that all coaches, athletes and parents involved buy-in to and support, you can create great teams that flourish, enabling young athletes to grow and thrive! And let's be honest, it makes your experience that much better as a coach.

REVIEW

Leave a Review

With everything you need to improve the mental toughness of your team and athletes right here, it's time to pass on your love for your game and show other coaches where they can find the same help.

Reviews are the lifeblood of an author. Simply by leaving your honest opinion of this book on Amazon, you'll show other coaches where they can find the information they're looking for, ready to improve their own skills and pass their passion for the sport forward. Thank you for your help. The game is kept alive when we pass on our knowledge – and you're helping me to do just that.

http://Amazon.com/review/create-review?&asin=B0CL3J9 R16

How to Teach Mental Skill Review Link

Q&A with Coaches

Q1: How do you get them to lower their expectations? I believe so many of my players have such high expectations.

This question is important, as it shows the contrast between seeking excellence and seeking perfection. Striving for perfection is never productive. It is unattainable and leads to more problems with confidence, self-esteem, etc. than it helps. I think helping them be more realistic, instead of "lowering their expectations", is more helpful. Giving up high or unrealistic expectations is difficult for young players. In these cases, adding to or expanding their definition of success is essential.

For example, I had a basketball player I was working with recently who was really struggling. At the beginning of the season, she was scoring a lot. She's a shooter, but towards the latter half of the season, she was getting really frustrated, because she wasn't scoring as much as the beginning of the season. Scoring was her sole measure of success as an athlete then. What she wasn't considering is that other teams started defending her differently because of her scoring skills. She now had less opportunity to score because she was being double teamed, triple teamed, etc. What really worked for her was helping her expand, not change, her definition of success.

She still wanted to score a lot of points. But we added to her definition of success with things like the number of rebounds, hustling to play defense, assists, that kind of thing. By helping athletes consider more than just one factor for success, they can avoid perfectionism.

And it doesn't hurt to remind them that, especially with softball and baseball, perfection is literally impossible. Doing everything right and hitting the ball hard doesn't always mean you'll get a hit. As a coach, in your own language, reinforce proper expectations, that are effort and execution based expectations. For example, did they do the parts that they can control right? If they did great, whatever happened as the outcome is out of their control.

Coaches can help athletes by adding process-related goals to expand their definition of success.

Q2: Can you coach parents to understand expectations in a procedural way so it's consistent the entire season? E.g. rating team toughness, etc.

Yes, you can. It can be difficult. While most parents genuinely want what's best for their kids, they don't always agree with you and what that is. However, it all starts with whatever culture you set as the coach at the beginning of the season. In youth sports, the parents get a vote on their child's experience. Manage expectations and work hard to align with parents according to the level of play you are coaching. If you coach a developmental team, you need to clarify playtime expectations and how you'll rotate players through positions.

Everything starts with clear and consistent communication between coach and parents. Be as clear as you can with the parents on what to expect from the level of team that you're coaching for. If it's an elite team, maybe those decisions differ from a developmental team.

The best option is to have clear and consistent communication. Unfortunately, as with all communication, the other person doesn't always react or respond the way you'd prefer. Make sure you set clear boundaries about what is and is NOT acceptable for parents as it relates to communicating with you and stick to your guns.

If a parent is consistently harassing you or breaking the "acceptable" rules for whatever reason, you might have to ask/request they leave the team. Maybe they're not the right fit for your team. Which happens from time to time. It can be a tough conversation to have, but ultimately might be best for everyone involved.

I always recommend coaches actually engage in the Discovery, Build Apply process as well. You all have your own opinions and perspectives on the sport, the kids you coach, the parents, the umpires, etc. After a tough conversation with a parent, ask yourself: "What did I learn today about myself and my reactions? Are my expectations of the situation appropriate or helpful? Did I approach it the best way I could?"

Q3: How do you help an athlete be more consistent? I have a player that will make a few great pitches, then come back and make a bunch of bad ones.

Sound mechanics and technique contribute to overall consistency. It is very difficult to achieve consistency without being able to repeat an action or enact a series of mechanical steps correctly. Building muscle memory and neural pathways through deliberate practice is the first step to consistency. You must first build the muscle memory.

Once you take care of that, you can shift to the mental side of consistency, which, I'm sure is no surprise, involves mindset and focus.

Often, what happens in sports is that athletes fall into the **gambler's fallacy.**

Let's say that I had a coin, and I was flipping it and I want you to guess heads or tails. I'm going to do it ten times and your goal is to guess correctly as often as possible. The coin landed on heads for the first five throws. On the sixth throw, humans rely on past information. For example, it's been heads five times, therefore it's going to be tales next. When in reality, nothing about the previous iterations determines the next toss. The toss is 50/50, regardless of what happened previously.

The gambler's fallacy is the belief that past events affect the probability of future random events. While throwing a good pitch or having the ball hit in your direction isn't exactly that same as a random event, athletes still used this biased idea to determine what will happen next when playing sports.

Players make flawed assumptions based on past events. i.e., the last few pitches I threw were off target. Therefore, the next one will be too. In basketball, I was very successful at scoring in the first two quarters of the basketball game. Therefore, I will keep sinking buckets for the rest of the game. Technically, these previous attempts have no bearing on the right now, the next shot I'm taking or the next pitch I'm making.

Help players control what they can control to influence consistency and avoid the gambler's fallacy. Help them recognize that each pitch or each play is completely separate from any play that's happened prior. Focus on doing your best now, without letting past attempts affect you.

The biggest thing you can do in my perspective is just help them wash the slate clean, so whatever happened prior gets flushed away. Help them focus on the right here right now, this next play, this next pitch and what will help them make the best possible pitch/play now. Focus on what's going to help them make the best pitch possible for this next pitch.

It's also important to note that your own reactions as the coach can impact your athlete. How do you breed consistency? Are you consistent in your own reactions, actions, etc? You don't want to be reactive, changing the way you yell, cheer, coach based on what is happening on the field.

You shouldn't have different expectations on game day than you do at practice. You shouldn't interact with your athletes differently just because you are frustrated with how the game is going.

Now, of course, you need to respond to real time game moments. You have tactics and coaching to do. These must be consistent in every game. You should give feedback in the same way whether you are losing by 10 or winning by 1 run in a tight game. Athletes take their cues from the coach. They feed off of your actions, reactions, words etc. Make sure you are consistent, so they know what to expect.

Q4: Regarding building trust between players, I've got players that play in a lot of different clubs teams that come together for high school. They tell me they play differently with their club team and I'm trying to figure out how to bring them all together to play for their future with this group at school.

There's no correct approach, but I've found that it helps to explain that it's alright if their club team does things differently. But they need to acknowledge that here on this team, we do things a certain way.

Gather all athletes and create a team culture by using the Great Team's exercise from the previous chapter.

Unfortunately, trust takes time. It's a developmental thing that requires shared experiences and shared struggle. Create scenarios in your practices where they must rely on each other to succeed. It could be some sort of drill where one team member cannot be successful without everybody else in their group pulling their weight. You can either choose regular team-building activities or make up your own games that include baseball/softball drills with team-focused twists.

One thing I've found that works well is incorporating blindfolds. Take away someone's vision and make them rely on a teammate to complete a task. Now, as tempting as it might be, don't hit or throw balls at people who can't see. :-) You can do something like having athletes partner up to navigate through a field littered with equipment. The partner wearing the blindfold needs to listen to their buddy's instructions to avoid stepping on equipment in the field.

You could even use the accoutabilibuddy system to have teammates teach each other something. Partner people up that have different strengths and have them coach each other on the thing that they're really strong at. Ultimately, you want to create shared experiences and opportunities for players to get to know each other and you. Involve yourself and the coaching staff in team-building activities.

RESOURCES

Confident, Calm and Clutch: How to Build Confidence and Mental Toughness for Athletes Using Sports Psychology (Mental Strength Books For Teens and Their Parents Book 1)

Purchase Individual copies from Amazon.com

Purchase multiple copies at a 33% discount for your team by using the QR Code Below

Audio Version: Available from Amazon and Audible.com

****

Confident, Calm & Clutch Journal: Your Mental Toughness Training Companion (Mental Strength Books For Teens and Their Parents)

Purchase individual copies from Amazon.com

Purchase multiple copies of the journal at a 33% discount for your team by using the QR Code below

Worksheets

- Book club homework

- PPP Worksheet

- Book Recommendations

https://www.valstoncoaching.com/coach-companion-resources

Coach's Corner Community

Website: https://www.valstoncoaching.com/3-cs-book-coaches

All links can be found by scanning this QR code

WHAT OTHERS HAVE TO SAY ABOUT THE CONFIDENT, CALM AND CLUTCH BOOKS

***5.0 out of 5 stars* Youth baseball player**I'm the mama to a youth baseball player. I've watched my son (and his team!) struggle with the mental part of baseball this season. I picked this up as a way to learn more about how I could maybe help with the mental aspect of the game. This was an easy read and I picked up some things to have my son try.

5.0 out of 5 stars **Great book!**Great book, straightforward and easy to read! My kids felt better playing their sports after we read the book as a family and they were able to recognize areas that they need more work. Happy we purchased this book!

5.0 out of 5 stars **Excellent read for young athletes and their families**Reviewed in the United States on June 2, 2023**Verified Purchase**I wish I would've had this book when I was in middle and high school as an introverted scholar athlete. I appreciated the real-life examples incorporated throughout. The book is authentically written and the author's witty sense of humor shines through. I highly recommend this book for young athletes and their parents/guardians.

5.0 out of 5 stars **Incredible Read!**If you are an athlete, parent, coach, or instructor...this is a must read! I pride myself of getting to know my athletes and what makes them say and do the things they do. This book has not only helped me become a better coach, it has also helped me understand my own self better. The first time I read the book from the perspective of my daughters or what I thought their perspective would be. As I reread chapters again, I find myself relating it to my own experiences. This is a great source of information and it is very well written! Kudos to Valerie for the time, energy, and effort she puts into helping others!

5.0 out of 5 stars **Excellent**Highly recommended! Well written and really helps me support my daughter through this high pressure process. My daughter loves the real life examples.

5.0 out of 5 stars **Must Read**Great book for athletes and sport psychology professionals! I really liked how there were concrete tools to utilize today and real-life examples to really understand the importance of training your mind. If you're not sure where to start in mental training or how to teach it, this is the book for you!

5.0 out of 5 stars LOVE this book!Reviewed in the United States on March 17, 2023**Verified Purchase**I wish I had the funds to buy this book for my whole team! I couldn't put this book down. I found each chapter useful to coaching and encouraging my athletes to become a better version of themselves. I definitely plan on incorporating these mindfulness drills into our season. Thank you for sharing your knowledge. (Special Note from Val: I have a discount program for coaches to do just this on the resource page)

5.0 out of 5 stars **Great Read!**Excellent read for parents, coaches, and players. Real world experience from the author/former player makes the book. The drills and tips provided are explained well and blended with stories to keep the reader engaged.
Recommended.

5.0 out of 5 stars Terrific Resource for teens AND parents!Valerie does a great job distilling evidence based sport psychology tools in an accessible way for teens to improve their game and parents to help support the development of mental toughness for their teens!

5.0 out of 5 stars **Page Turner!**As a parent this book was amazing in understanding daughter and how to help her improve I'm her craft! It might show a baseball on the cover page, but this is for any sport.

5.0 out of 5 stars **Great book**This is a great read for young athletes and coaches. She gives proven techniques to develop the mental game and thoroughly explains how and why these techniques work.

4.0 out of 5 stars **Good read for young athletes!**A good read geared towards high school softball players, providing them strategies to becoming a mentally tough player from life experiences of a former player. At times the author comes off in a way that reads that applying the mental techniques will guarantee success without reminding that the reader still needs to put in the physical work to expect successful results. Nonetheless it would be a good read for any young softball player to gain techniques in being a better player and overall person with strategies to help them cope with mentally challenging times and situations.

5.0 out of 5 stars **Great for coaches, parents, players**Reviewed in the United States on May 15, 2023I have been coaching assorted sports for 20 years, and am now coaching my daughters 12U softball team. I got through this book and instantly knew that I was going to have my daughter read the book, and/or walk her through the concepts that help with mental toughness. Valerie does a great job of making the book very readable for all ages. This book is a great resource for both boy and girls.

***5.0 out of 5 stars* The best information for ball players , pro and new**This book is great for any player , from college age to those just starting out ! I'm reading as a parent And Coach so I can help not only my daughter - should she choose to pursue a career in softball or my players (and also mental toughness for myself) this book is filled with wonderful ideas , some taken from real life experiences. You won't be disappointed!

***5.0 out of 5 stars* Mental Toughness**Reviewed in the United States on April 16, 2023This book is a blue print for anyone trying to create the mental toughness it takes to take on challenges head on. It simplifies the process of coping with the pains and strains it takes to compete on any walk of life. I would highly recommend this book to any young reader who is coping with the stress and anxieties it takes to compete in such a competitive world.